THE UNFLAWED LEADER

CREATING A CULTURE OF CHRISTLIKE
WELLNESS IN THE LOCAL CHURCH

STAN O. GLEASON

ISBN 978-1-68517-663-1 (paperback)
ISBN 978-1-68517-664-8 (digital)

Christian Faith Publishing
832 Park Avenue
Meadville, PA 16335
www.christianfaithpublishing.com

Scriptures marked NKJV are taken from the NEW KING JAMES VERSION (NKJV): Scripture taken from the NEW KING JAMES VERSION®. Copyright© 1982 by Thomas Nelson, Inc. Used by permission. All rights reserved.

Other versions used:
NIV © 2021 Biblica
NLT © 2007
GW (God's Word) © 2020
TLB © 1971
CEV (Contemporary English Version) © 1995 American Bible Society
NLV (New Life Version) © 1969, 2003 Barbour Publishing
NASB © 2020 The Lockman Foundation

Printed in the United States of America

Stacy
Hankins
March-2023

He has done all things well (Mark 7:37).

37 And were beyond astonished, Saying, He hath done all things well: he maketh both the deaf to hear, and the dumb to speak.

DEDICATION

T his book is lovingly dedicated to my wife, the Queen Marlene. Together we have raised four passionate Christ followers who serve together in our local church. The family that follows the wellness model of Jesus Christ together stays together.

CONTENTS

INTRODUCTION

Anyone can love the perfect church, but the challenge is to love the real one. If you find the perfect church, please don't join it because you'll ruin everything. Job said that it only takes a few days of living in this world for a man's soul to be full of trouble, and it takes a few worship services to find something you don't like about a local church. I've met a few folks who didn't need that many.

The church business is the most unique enterprise on Earth. A local congregation is comprised of people from all walks of life who are captured by the vision of the pastor who is being paid by this volunteer army to put *them* to work. What an idea! More than anyone, the pastor stands to gain or lose from every single action or word he performs. How wonderful it would be if all four hundred thousand congregations in America were led by flawless pastors and attended by perfect people. The church is not a museum of stuffed and mounted perfect leaders and followers, but is more like a hospital and in some cases a MASH unit, where broken, wounded, and dying victims from the ravages of this world can find recovery, healing, and hope.

Hurting people enter hospitals to be treated for one issue, but on occasion contact a disease more dangerous while a patient under care. If you have never been wounded in the house of God you are exceptional, not normal. The question is not, "Are you going to be hurt?" You will be hurt, so have a nice day. But the question is, "What are you going to do with the hurt?" You can receive the hurt, take it in, become offended, and walk away from your only hope in this world. Or you can forgive and confront with redemption as the goal, and not cheat yourself out of being a vital part of God's mission in the world.

An Old Testament priestly garment would cost ten thousand dollars to recreate today, but the man who wore it in the Tabernacle was commanded by God to walk in bare feet. This was a reminder by God to his representative that he was a flawed man, and at the end of the day when he hung up his regal robes, there would be dirt between his toes. I have often told our congregation not to look too closely at my life for they are sure to find something that might disappoint them. I have nothing to hide; I am not living in sin; and I am not ashamed of how I live, spend money, or use my leisure time, but scrutiny exposes flawed flesh.

I agreed to join a church staff when the pastor promised to transition the congregation to my leadership in "two to three years" (if I did a good job and everything was working out well). We added value to everything we touched, and created new ministries beyond our initial job description that edified the congregation and impacted the community. After three years, not one word had been said about my future. One day as I was talking with the pastor, I decided to ask him if his plans were the same for a transition. There were many things he could have said that I would have been okay with, but he uttered the only thing I could not bear: "I don't remember saying anything about handing the church to you in two to three years."

His wife and my wife were sitting in the room when he dangled that carrot. However, I did not press the issue and call in the witnesses. I decided in that moment that I could not follow a man who did not honor his word. I proceeded to tell him that I was tendering my thirty-day notice of resignation. A few days later, while we were out of town for Christmas vacation, he read our letter of resignation to the congregation (written by him), and we were never allowed to attend another service before we left town.

This entire episode was a bitter disappointment but also an eye-opener. My biggest takeaway was a determination to never repeat this mistake with a staff member if I ever became a pastor. Ironically, three years later he reached out to me after his wife was diagnosed with terminal cancer. In tears, he said he knew he could trust me and was ready now to turn the church over to me. I asked him who would be making the financial decisions (that's who's in charge)? He said that we would "work that out" after I got there. I saw a repeat performance in my future, so I declined the opportunity. Every leader has blind spots, but discovering them is an eye-opener.

How would you describe the culture of your local church? Church culture entails the collective attitude, environment, setting, health, personality, and dynamics in play that create a unique gathering of believers. Elder Johnny James said, "If you think one church is just like another church, you'd probably think King Kong was just another monkey." Culture happens—whether intentionally or unintentionally—in homes, corporations, churches, and other entities. Church culture is primarily fostered by the pastor who leads it, and secondarily by the faithful members who call it home. Therefore, it is easy to see how one congregation is unlike any other.

While it is true that without a vision the people perish, it is also true that without a supporting culture the vision will perish. Culture feeds on vision. Vision tells you where you want to go, but culture takes you there. In January the pastor can preach an outstanding message about the vision for the coming year, but if the culture in that church does not support the vision, it will quickly fade. Too many pastors become frustrated when their vision-casting messages don't take root in the daily lives of the congregants. The strategic leader knows that vision leaks, so it must be spoken continually and creatively. Perhaps most important, the vision also must be modeled by the leader(s), because people do not do what they hear leaders say; they do what they see leaders do.

Leaders who personally model their vision will impact their local church culture. J. T. Pugh said, "Whatever is in the heart of the pastor will come out in the congregation." Whether or not pastors want to admit it, they are the greatest influencers in the local church. The personality, spirit, persona, values, and attitude of the pastor will eventually trickle down into the leadership team and ultimately infiltrate every fiber of the congregation. This reality has personally alarmed me on numerous occasions, particularly when I have not been at my best. I understand that I, as a pastor, will not attract what

I want, but only what I am. Charles de Gaulle said, "History does not teach fatalism… People get the history they deserve."

Daniel Webster said, "My highest thought is my individual responsibility to God." Standing before God and giving an account of a ministerial life is an ominous consideration. Some frustrated church leaders occasionally feel compelled to remind their followers that one day they will stand before God and give an account for their poor behavior. The bigger issue, however, is that all church leaders, including licensed ministers, departmental heads, teachers, and parents will give an account of how well they have modeled the behavior they desire to reproduce in those God has entrusted to their care.

A church leader's self-examination should include questions like: Am I giving God a return for his considerable investment of resources in me? Is everything I'm touching healthy? Is it going to a new level? Am I adding value to everything I'm leading? Am I sufficiently equipping, training, modeling, and empowering those I'm leading? Am I creating a nonthreatening environment suitable for experimentation, growth, and development? Am I presenting Christlike wellness, balance, and appropriateness in every conversation and relationship? Do the people I lead feel better or worse about themselves after being in my presence?

There are many leadership models in the kingdom of God. When we think of models, we typically think of styles of leadership. This book is not about a style of leadership but rather an examination of the basis for a style of leadership. The foundation of leadership is deeper than style because it resounds down to the bedrock of the leader's motivation. The heart ultimately reveals what inspires and regulates leaders and how their interaction with those they lead is presented. Presentation is everything. I enjoy a good steak, but I don't want anyone shoving it down my throat. Paul said if we are "speaking the truth in love," then we are fostering a culture conducive to developing full spiritual maturity (Eph. 4:15), which should be every church leader's ultimate goal.

Sometimes we look at leaders and wonder what makes them tick. Why do leaders do what they do? And after they have said or done it, did we learn anything? Was it profitable? Did it bear fruit?

But speaking the truth in love, may grow up into him in all things, which is the head, even Christ;

4

Did it edify, equip, or encourage? Or in the aftermath of the leader's action did it demoralize, defeat, discourage, disengage, or destroy? John Maxwell has often said, "He who thinks he's leading but has no one following is only taking a walk." Church leaders would do well to turn around occasionally and see if anyone is following them, and also examine the shape they are in.

In 1961 President John F. Kennedy boldly declared that before the end of the decade that America would put a man on the moon. A story has circulated for years about the president touring NASA sometime later. As he was being ushered by the Secret Service through the facility, he suddenly broke away, turned a corner, and walked a short distance down a hallway where he saw an employee mopping a floor. Kennedy asked him what he was doing. The worker replied, "Mr. President, we are putting a man on the moon." Now that is culture. When the guy mopping the floor miles away from the launch pad feels part of the big picture, that is something special.

I was a saint before I was a pastor. I have sat on both sides of the altar—the pew and the platform. I have witnessed both excellent and poor church leadership. I have sat in groups of church leaders and listened to them talk about some of the folks in their congregation. Their descriptions can range from "my amazing church" to "that bunch I pastor." I once heard a pastor quip (tongue-in-cheek): "I love pastoring, it's the people I hate." But in this work, my heart goes out to good-hearted, honest, well-meaning church members who perhaps did not have the assumed advantage of sitting under healthy, well-balanced, kingdom-minded leadership.

This is a book about wellness in church leadership. It's possible, it's the expectation, it's what leaders and congregations sign up for, but it doesn't always happen. Books aplenty have been written about church leaders who lead with a limp, lead with pain, lead on empty, and lead a purpose-driven church. But I've known good humble saints who walked with a limp, followed in pain, obeyed on empty, and were driven more like cattle than led like sheep. This is usually the case when the undershepherd they trusted with their soul was himself broken and failed to follow in the steps of the great shepherd, Jesus Christ.

An elder minister and friend of mine told a story about one of the many trips he hosted to the Holy Land. One day on a tour bus with his group, he looked out the window and noticed a shepherd and his flock. He had seen many typical scenes depicting benevolent shepherds leading contented flocks, but this was different. This shepherd was yelling, beating, kicking, and cursing the sheep. He went so far as to snatch up a stray lamb and cast it back into the flock.

My friend asked the driver to stop the bus. He stepped out and approached the shepherd. Having a working knowledge of the Hebrew language, he said to the man, "I've been to Israel many times and seen many shepherds interacting with their flock. I must confess that I've never seen a shepherd treat his sheep like you do. I watched you kick and scream at them, and even throw them around. What kind of a shepherd are you?" The man looked at him and with a shrug and said, "I'm not the shepherd, I'm the butcher."

Church leaders occasionally bog down in the morass of people problems or their own personal pain. In addition, it's not uncommon for a church leader's actions or attitudes to become tainted by bad personal habits and unresolved hurts and hang-ups. An unhealthy leader will have difficulty imitating the model of the ultimate leader presented to us by the four Gospel evangelists.

God chose the model he wanted the leaders of his church to emulate. Jeremiah 3:15 (NLT) says, "I will give you shepherds after my own heart, who will guide you with knowledge and understanding." He did not give his people policemen, dictators, tyrants, or lords over his heritage. None of these models would be found in the heart of God. His desired model was clearly demonstrated in the ultimate, perfect leader, Jesus Christ.

This work is a biblically based perspective of the leadership culture of wellness that Jesus established among his closest followers. He was intentional with every word, action, and attitude that he modeled among his disciples. Jesus was the ultimate leader; but better than that, he was the only flawless leader in human history who brought no baggage, no scars, no wounds, no hang-ups, no hurts, no habits, no unresolved emotional issues, and no dysfunction to his leadership team.

At the beginning of each chapter, we will attempt to identify moments in biblical text when Jesus demonstrated the kind of leadership culture of wellness he wanted his trainees (and all of us) to follow. He never had to apologize, take back his words, or patch up a relationship gone wrong because of him. He never deceived, manipulated, broke trust, betrayed confidence, pitched a childish fit, used guilt motivation, or staged a colossal meltdown. He did all things well (Mark 7:37).

We will honor God and his word—and benefit ourselves and those we lead—if we will consistently revisit the wellness model of leadership embodied by Christ as he was forging his church on this earth. In a mere forty-two months, he called, chose, trained, empowered, and released a team of leaders who faithfully adhered to his wellness model. He was so successful in reproducing his attitude in his team that even the detractors of the disciples later marveled and acknowledged that they were acting and speaking just like Jesus (Acts 4:13).

There is only one church, and there is only one pastor of that church, "that great shepherd of the sheep" (Heb. 13:20, KJV). At best, any lead pastor, senior pastor, or staff pastor of a local church is an undershepherd of the Great Shepherd. May Jesus step out of the ink and paper of the Bible, and may the Spirit of Christ direct us to follow his steps. Together we are invited to imitate Jesus and recreate his model of wellness in our local church leadership.

Now when they saw the boldness of Peter and John, and percieved that they were unlearned and ignorant men, they marvelled; and they took knowledge of them, that they had been with Jesus.

Now the God of peace, that brought again from the dead of our lord Jesus, that great Shepherd of the sheep, through the blood of the everlasting Covenant.

CHAPTER 1

CHRISTLIKE LEADERS MUST DIE

Most assuredly, I say to you, unless a grain of wheat falls into the ground and dies, it remains alone; but if it dies, it produces much grain (John 12:24).

"You can't keep a good man down, and you can't keep a bad man up."—Unknown

I do not hold a qualified degree in behavioral science and claim no expertise or professional achievement in this area. However, I graduated summa cum laude from the school of hard knocks, as well as negotiating numerous experiences in handling broken people throughout forty-three years in full-time ministry. I have also learned priceless but expensive lessons in every seasonal transition of my life and ministry.

I was called by God into the ministry on the evening of August 5, 1976. That moment was so vivid that forty-four years later I can take you to the place, and I can recall all the details: those who were in that small-group prayer meeting, the desk and chairs in the pastor's office, the voices of prayer around me. In the holy moment of that call, among other things, God clearly spoke these momentous words to me: "I will use you in healings of the mind, the soul, and the body."

For a long time, I interpreted that word from the Lord in a generic sense, realizing that all called men and women of God are used to bring healing and restoration to the broken people around them. It was not until I had been in full-time ministry for ten years that I clearly understood that God had spoken this to me particularly and not generically.

I came to the congregation we have served the last thirty-three years as a broken church leader. Nearly six years prior to this new ministry venture, my wife and I had suffered a barrage of criticism and spiritual attack while serving out a ministry assignment. Strangely enough, despite a chronically excruciating season of attempting to lead a dysfunctional congregation back to the wellness model of Jesus, I wept profusely while trying to unpack my resignation announcement during my last Sunday sermon. That was in November of 1987. On July 10, 1988, we were elected pastor of Life Tabernacle (now the Life Church) in Kansas City, Missouri.

During our nine-month season between pastorates, I came to the end of myself, and for the first time in my life I faced hopelessness. I felt spiritually lost and professionally bankrupt. The years of abuse in the ministry had taken their toll and left me disillusioned about God, my calling, and my future. It was only the grace of God and the kindness of the invitations of pastor friends that I was earning a living. One night at a ministers' conference I scheduled three months of meetings, but when I got back to my hotel room, I slammed my little black book on the desk and angrily told myself, "You idiot. Now you have to go and preach at all those places."

It is a fearful thing to know you've been called but have no desire move forward. My wife and I discussed resigning from the ministry, choosing a city, applying for "real jobs," finding a church, being good church members, and raising our children to serve the Lord. Perhaps the only reason I had not already quit is because I had no trade or career to fall back on. The only thing I had been trained for was the ministry, so I was stuck. Preaching had become a means to pay the bills, so I just kept on clanging like an unmanned machine.

The first glimmer of hope came on a cold Sunday morning in February in Albion, Michigan. I had met the pastor only the day before, the connection being that my cousin—also a pastor—was this man's brother-in-law. My weekend engagement had been canceled, but God quickly ordered this opened door in Albion. As I sat on the platform during the worship, the congregation began to sing "Jesus, you're everything to me. You have provided all my needs. When I thought there was no way, you led me to a brighter day. Jesus you're everything to me." It sounded like a choir of angels. I cannot adequately express the feeling that overwhelmed me.

I typically am undemonstrative, but suddenly I found myself face down on the carpet in the presence of God. The pastor knelt beside me and prophetically spoke Psalm 31:7–8 into my ear: "I will be glad and rejoice in Your mercy, for You have considered my trouble; You have known my soul in adversities, and have not shut me up into the hand of the enemy; You have set my feet in a wide place." This was my first glimmer of hope, but not my last fight with despair.

It has been said that we can live forty days without food, four days without water, and four minutes without oxygen, but we cannot live four seconds without hope. I still had some dark days ahead, but through that very personal message, I began to believe that perhaps God still had a plan for my life.

On June 5, 1988, I was a guest speaker in Lonoke, Arkansas. I intuitively knew that something was desperately wrong inside of me, and I understood that a calling was supposed to empower you through tough times, but I had nothing. I remember wondering if that was what it felt like to be lost and without God in this world. I was praying in the evangelist's quarters before the Sunday service, so disappointed and empty inside that my emotions boiled over, unleashing an angry prayer: "God, I'm not leaving this room until you give me a *desire* to do so!"

I crumpled to the floor, suit, tie, and all, sobbing uncontrollably. I'm not sure if I was in the Spirit or just feeling sorry for myself. Within a few minutes, I suddenly heard in my spiritual ear a still, small voice say, "First Corinthians 15:10." I had no idea what that verse said, but I quickly pawed through my Bible, trying to see through my tears: "But by the grace of God, I am what I am, and His grace toward me was not in vain." Then the voice came again: "Philippians 2:13." I raced to that verse: "For it is God who works in you both to will and to do for His good pleasure."

Instantly, I felt virtue infuse my mind, spirit, and body. I realized I had just received a personal revelation of the grace of God—that grace was his agent of spiritual desire at work in me. Up to that point I had ignorantly thought his grace was only the vehicle of my salvation, but the rest was up to me. I hadn't realized he not only was capable of giving me the desire to do what he wanted me to do, but he also was eager to give me the power to do it. Since that moment I have never been the same, and Philippians 2:13 has become my life verse.

This was a game-changer. I charged out of that room and stormed into the sanctuary, champing at the bit to preach. I hadn't felt empowered like this in months, if ever. I am a "note preacher," but all I had that night was two verses of scripture, a revelation, and a testimony. As I began to preach, I felt as though I had been shot out of a cannon. Those poor people never knew what hit them, and neither did I exactly. I lamented my journey but rejoiced in my revelation all over that sanctuary.

At the end of the service, an elder came to me and said tearfully, "Young man, I've been in the church my entire life but I've never heard or felt anything like what I did tonight." Then he gave me a "holy handshake." In his clasp was a pressed, crisp, folded piece of paper, which, upon subsequent eager inspection, turned out to be a check for seventy-five dollars. That may not seem like much to you, but in 1988, given the occasion, it felt like seven thousand five hundred dollars!

When things calmed down, a woman came up to my wife and me and said, "I don't know what this means, but in three weeks, God is going to give you direction for your ministry." Three weeks from that day I was preaching my first message in the congregation I now serve. When God decides to turns a person's captivity, it doesn't take him long to do it. When the student is ready, the teacher will appear.

But even that prophetic word did not seem to perfectly unfold. The board of directors told me they were going to consider another minister first. That was confusing, but I had no choice other than to trust God. In the meantime, a church overseer called me and asked if I would consider serving a congregation in Michigan. My wife and I and two small children drove seven hundred miles to minister to those people who needed a pastor. The situation appeared to be everything we were looking for, but after the service we both knew it was not the place God wanted. We were so disappointed, but that evening we received the call that we had been elected pastor of the congregation in Kansas City.

During our first eighteen months in our new assignment, fourteen families of our faith moved into town and began attending the church. For our small congregation, this was a significant increase. At first, I thought we were simply recipients of the favor of God. After all, these were mature, tithe-paying families in Christ who could begin helping us immediately. I typically do not ask new attendees a lot of questions but allow them to offer any part of their story they decide to share. It soon became apparent that their presence in our congregation was much more than God's bounty.

As they began to share their stories, I noticed a common thread: each of these families had come to us broken, disillusioned, and discouraged. They were smiling on the outside but distraught on the inside. They had not suffered from the ravages of sin; they had been wounded in the house of God. As I listened to them, my mind would often go to the story in 1 Samuel 22 about the four hundred distressed, debt-ridden, discontented men who came to David's hideout in the cave Adullam. David understood these men because of the brokenness and rejection he had suffered at the hands of Saul. Over time these men became part of his fierce fighting force called "David's Mighty Men" (2 Sam. 23).

For many months, I could not seem to finish a message without weeping at some point in the presentation. At first, I was embarrassed and upset at myself for being such a wimp. I could not bear listening to manipulative communicators, and I was afraid this was how I was coming across. Looking back, however, I believe God was healing my spirit through tears, vulnerability, and transparency while at the same time building trust toward spiritual leadership in the hearts of the wounded.

It was during this season that God showed me an imagery of two rectangular gardens situated side by side. Everything planted in the garden on the left seemed to have been trampled to some degree. Then I saw two hands come down and pluck up the damaged shrubs and flowers one by one, and gently transplant them in the garden on the right. Nothing in the garden on the right was perfect, but everything was clearly healing and growing again.

At the end of this presentation from the Lord, I heard the words of Isaiah 42:3, "A bruised reed He will not break, and smoking flax He will not quench." This was followed by a stern warning: "You have been damaged at the hands of toxic church people, but these I have sent to you have been broken by flawed church leadership. You should understand each other well. Your assignment is to rebuild their trust in spiritual leaders and faith in the mission of my church. This is their last chance. If you fail, they will be lost." God certainly knew how to capture my attention!

Through the years, many have come damaged and bruised but eventually have sprung up and recovered their faith and trust. Some were healed and have gone out from us to do great things for God; others have stayed and become a vital part of the healing process for countless others. At first, we were intentional about ministering to the spiritually downtrodden, but eventually the ministry of spiritual and emotional healing seeped into our spiritual DNA, and now it just seems to happen through "spiritual osmosis." We continually hear comments and witness changes that testify to this dynamic at work. To God be the glory! Recently a middle-aged couple who moved across the country to attend our church told me that the final work of healing and recovery happened the previous Sunday. Then they informed me they were moving back home. Mission accomplished.

Good church people can be in an unhealthy spiritual community and not even realize it, at least not at first. In 2005 we began construction on our new worship facility. I was forty-eight years old and had been healthy my entire life. During the thirteen months of the building process, however, I gradually noticed that I was feeling unwell. I assumed it was a combination of the stress of raising money, accumulating construction debt, and the daily rigors of construction.

Although I still was functional, I made an appointment to see my doctor, who diagnosed a case of hypertension. This condition runs in my family, so it was not a surprise. He prescribed a low-dose medication, and instantly I began to feel better. To this day my hypertension is still a concern, but it is under control.

The point is that I did not realize how badly I was feeling until I started feeling better. Looking back, I had been in bad shape for a long time without realizing it. The bad feeling had gradually crept up on me until one day I knew something was wrong, and I needed to take action.

Perhaps this illustration describes what happens to unhealthy church leaders and their followers. Everybody senses something is wrong, but since they are functional and some good things are happening, they feel no immediate cause for alarm.

When I was in kindergarten my parents introduced my siblings and I to "Chico" (our new little Mexican Chihuahua puppy). He came from a breeder and was accustomed to sharing his food bowl with other puppies. He would step up to his bowl, take a bite of food, and then step aside and wait for others to be served. It took him a few days of feedings to realize that was no longer necessary in his new home. It has been special to watch believers come from other places and discover their healthy new normal. They can step into the pastor's office without being scolded. They feel better, and not worse, upon leaving a worship service. They are now inspired by grace and not guilt. What a life, what a church, what a Christ?

The pattern of recovery usually consists of relief, debrief, forgive, healing, recovery, appreciation for a healthy church culture, rebirth of trust in leadership, and serving with gratitude. Please understand that I am not bragging, boasting, or attempting to set myself up as a hero. God knows I have suffered enough to never be seduced by the applause or accolades of adoring church members. But it is pure joy

We are of God: he that knoweth God heareth us; he that is not of God heareth not us. Hereby know we the spirit of truth, and the spirit of error.

to see hurting people spring up, believe, trust, and serve the kingdom of God with renewed liberty.

In 1 John 4:6 the apostle references "the spirit of error." The spirit of error has enough truth to make it seem right, but it's half a bubble off plumb theologically, relationally, or spiritually. Truth is not a club or weapon to be used by church leaders to penalize, intimidate, or manipulate. Jesus said that if believers know the truth, it will make them free (John 8:32).

And ye shall know the truth, and the truth shall make you free.

Truth is more than correct theology. A leader can preach perfect theology and have error in their spirit. The error could have sprung from offense, anger, the sheer force of human intimidation, manipulation, condemnation, guilt, or similar causes. The church member in the audience can be saying "amen" with their mouth, but feeling like "oh no" in their spirit. They know something is not right but they can't seem to put their finger on it. They understand they are to respect spiritual authority and they love the truth, but they are confused by the error.

I heard of a pastor who was an avid NFL football fan and passionately rooted for his favorite team every Sunday afternoon. The joke in the congregation was that if his team won that afternoon, his message in the evening service would be joyful, upbeat, and encouraging. But woe unto that congregation if the team lost because there would be hell to pay. It's a sad reality that many good church people have had to put up with petty defeats, poor attitudes, and human error spewing from leaders dealing with their own unresolved emotional issues.

The most powerful tool communicators have is their spirit. They can read a great text, transmit a revelatory idea, present a timeless truth, and share an interesting story, but if their heart isn't right with God and their fellowman, the spirit of error will poison the message. Paul said, "I always try to live so my own heart tells me I am not guilty before God or man" (Acts 24:16, NLV).

In the early 1990s I became entangled in a debate within our ministerial organization, which was my first mistake. I felt I was right (and still do), but my problem was that I entertained a spirit of offense, which was my second mistake. My third mistake was that

I took "preacher talk" to the pulpit. Over the next few months my offended spirit leaked out into the innocent congregation. I had never done this before and have never done it since. It was a hard lesson to learn.

At a ministers' conference about six months later, I was severely reprimanded by the Lord in prayer. I made my heart right with my leader in a face-to-face meeting during which a powerful prayer moment released forgiveness and healing into my spirit. The ultimate decision in our organization did not go my way, but I refrained from picking up that banner again.

At the first opportunity, I stood before our congregation and apologized for my offended spirit and poor attitude. Perhaps someone reading this right now may be thinking, "What a wimp. I would never apologize in front of my congregation." Well, you can go ahead and be a brute, but *you* know you were wrong, your members know, and God knows you are, so you might as well apologize and get it over with.

After my apology, one of the elders came up to me and said, "You became my pastor today. [I had been elected five years prior.] I knew something was wrong, but I didn't know what to do about it. I know you are a man of prayer, but I realized today that you are capable of being corrected by God, and I can follow a man like that."

Before truth is doctrine or a set of rules to live by, it is a man, a person, a life well-lived by our supreme example. John wrote that there is a "doctrine of Christ" (2 John 1:9 NKJV). Jesus said, "I am the truth." There is no spirit of error in either the human or divine nature of Jesus Christ. Paul said, "Have this attitude in yourselves which was also in Christ Jesus" (Phil. 2:5, NASB). Church leaders must be careful not to misrepresent Jesus Christ in any way to those who are following them. It is a fearful thing to lead in Christ's stead but not in his steps.

A leader can be doctrinally true, but his/her spirit can be in error. Our human spirit is more important in communication than rhetoric, polemic, sermonizing, or body language. For this reason, the greatest impartations from communicators are more caught than taught. Jesus warned us that in the last days there would be many

[handwritten margin note:] Whosoever trans-gresseth, and abideth not in the doctrine of Christ, hath not God. He that abideth in the doctrine of Christ, he hath both the father and the son.

17

false Christs. We tend to think of these imposters as infamous cult leaders, but more than one false Christ has stood behind a pulpit with a spirit not at all like his. There's a fine line between presenting the Jesus of the Gospels and the Jesus adjusted by human psychosis.

The psalmist said that God desires truth in the inward parts (Psa. 51:6). Perhaps this is what inspired him to then pray, "Create in me a clean heart, O God, and renew a right spirit within me" (Psa. 51:10, KJV). I often pray along with the psalmist, "Let the words of my mouth and the meditation of my heart be acceptable in Your sight, O Lord" (Psa. 19:14). The most powerful force in the world is the preaching of the truth of God's word, spoken through a clean vessel unadulterated by personal agenda or human error and received by a ready heart.

Paul, as a master communicator and writer, used every resource he had when addressing an unhealthy church situation at Corinth. The dysfunction at work has been well rehearsed. Scholars suggest that Paul wrote to them four times, but we only have access to letters two and four. In 1 Corinthians Paul argued for his apostleship over them and rebuked them for their divisions, misuse of spiritual gifts, and the open toleration of sexual sin.

To their credit, they had a change of heart and received Paul's correction, enabling him to write 2 Corinthians with joy. He explained, "But I determined this within myself, that I would not come again to you in sorrow. For if I make you sorrowful, then who is he who makes me glad but the one who is made sorrowful by me?" (2:1–2).

The greatest joy and source of edification of church leaders should be the people they lead. Years ago, I had a colleague that I could read like a book because his mood was determined by the way he felt at any given moment about the church he pastored. When it was good, he would call them, "Those beautiful people," but when it was bad, the expression became, "That bunch I got." Sometimes they were a beautiful bunch. I've often said that I can experience one hundred ministry-related disappointments, but one positive breakthrough action can wipe out all the bad.

Church members need correction at times, but not all the time. Paul understood that whatever he wanted or needed to come back to him as a leader, he first needed to send out to others. He explained that if he sent out sorrow, then that was what would come back to him, which the church at Corinth did in repentance. But in 2 Corinthians he desired encouragement, so he wrote to them with words of gladness. Leaders who think the only way to get action out of people is through condemnation or guilt motivation will have a difficult time staying encouraged themselves, because that is exactly the return they will receive.

I am deeply impressed by Paul's healthy leadership model as I read through 2 Corinthians. He informed them that he made no attempts to control them, but they had fenced themselves in by their lack of love-based motivation. He welcomed them into the spacious and expansive life of love and liberty (2 Cor. 6:11–13). In 2 Corinthians 7:2, he encouraged the believers to open their hearts to him and his leadership team (Titus). They previously had opened their hearts to rebelling against spiritual authority, division, and immorality, so he knew they understood how to open themselves up. But this subsequent opening was that of a healthy vulnerability toward spiritual authority. Church members cannot grow if they have erected walls against leadership. Paul argued that he had neither wronged, corrupted, nor cheated anyone, and this earned him the right to be trusted and followed.

Now consider the following seven consecutive statements that can only come out of the mouth (or pen) of a healthy leader:

1. I am not condemning you.
2. You are in my heart.
3. I will die or live with you.
4. I can speak boldly to you.
5. I boast to others about you.
6. Your lives fill me up with comfort.
7. I am joyful with you, even in hard times.

[handwritten margin notes: "O ye corinthians, our mouth is open unto you, our heart is enlarged. ye are not straitened in us but ye are straitened in your own bowels. Now for a recompence in the same (I speak as unto my children) be ye also enlarged." Left margin: "Recieve us", "we have", "wronged", "no man", "we have", "corrupted", "no man", "we have", "defrauded", "no man"]

19

In his Leadership Bible, John Maxwell demonstrates how leaders mete out either bad sorrow or good sorrow:

Bad Sorrow	Good Sorrow
Pain continues indefinitely	Pain is temporary
Example of Judas	Example of Peter
Leads to regret and death	Leads to repentance and life
Suffering based on selfishness	Suffering based on God's will

I'm convinced that most of the bad leadership models are rooted in unmet emotional issues. This may sound Freudian, but it stands to reason that *what* we go through and *how* we go through it impacts our future relationships. For a few years after I was elected pastor where I now serve, the phrase "board meeting" triggered a negative emotional response in my gut. During the five previous years in countless battlefield board meetings, I had been subjected to criticism, personal attacks, having my motives misjudged, or my leadership stereotyped. One board meeting was even called to terminate my service, but by the grace of God I survived the interrogation.

But just because those particular board members took exception to me personally, to my leadership, and to my office does not mean every church board is built the same way. Nevertheless, unhealthy emotions were triggered in me that I had to disassociate. I have never walked to a pulpit mad, I have never used my authority to crush or retaliate, and I have never manipulated anyone to my advantage and their disadvantage.

In thirty-seven years of pastoring, I have told only three men that it would be better for them if they found another house of worship. And that was only after painstaking attempts to administer care and offer resolution. None of them could say that I threw them away. The good news is that one of them followed my prescription for restoration and returned three years later. He is now a vital part of our congregation.

I'm quite certain that I am not a big enough or gifted enough leader to pastor everyone who visits our church. Our congregation is not the greatest church in the world, but I've said for years with tongue in cheek, "If you can't make it here, I'm not sure you can make it anywhere."

Most pastors feel tremendous pressure to grow their church. "Church growth" has become a marketable enterprise within Christianity by which some gifted writers and presenters have netted substantial sums of money. I have attended numerous church growth conferences through the years, but have often left confused and discouraged rather than equipped and inspired. I'm sure it is usually assumed by the speakers at growth conferences that they are communicating with healthy leaders. But they don't know these leaders and probably will never see them again. It would be refreshing to go to a growth conference just once where instead of everyone sharing their good stories, someone would get real and unveil mistakes they have made as leaders.

Church leaders' insecurities can drive them to succeed or to reach for recognition, but at what cost? For them arrival is everything, no matter who gets manipulated, taken for granted, or pushed aside in the process. Thirty years ago, a pastor spent ten thousand dollars on promoting and hosting a big prophecy weekend. Years later he told me he had absolutely nothing to show for it. I'm sure the volunteers worked hard to make it all happen, but what it amounted to was exhaustion, feeling used, and doubting the leader's judgment. Beyond that, it was a great morale reducer for the next ill-advised adventure.

I'm wondering what would happen if church leaders would focus on church wellness and not church growth; if their church offered wellness as its product instead of promotions, programs, prosperity, and popularity; if they spent less time on bigness and more on wellness; if every leader's home was well, every marriage in leadership was well, every ministry leader was well, and every department was highly functional but not in a hyperactive way.

Is there a better way? Paul thought so. He closed out 1 Corinthians 12 with a curious statement. He had just finished correcting this chaotic congregation by giving them controls that would restore proper order for the operation of the gifts of the Spirit. In chapter 11 he had indicted them for failing to discern the Lord's body in the moment of communion. Because of this egregious error they were experiencing unnecessary sickness, chronic spiritual anemia, and untimely deaths. Then he concluded chapter 12 with, "And yet I show you a more excellent way" (1 Cor. 13:31b).

Leadership was disjointed. The church members were following one of their four favorites: Paul, Apollos, Cephas, or Christ—who would you choose? Sexual immorality was perhaps not celebrated, but it was tolerated. Visitors were confused during worship services because of a lack of spiritual controls. Their selfish attitude during communion incurred destruction upon them. This local congregation was not well in any area of their operation. Some congregations at least can mask their brokenness by doing a few things reasonably well (like hospitality or music), but the Corinthians could be featured on a poster depicting a broken church. Fortunately for them—as well as for us—Paul outlined a more excellent way. If they would follow it, every dysfunction in operation within the Corinthian community would be corrected.

Our Bible is arranged in chapters and verses for greater ease in locating passages of scripture. But there were no chapters when Paul was writing under inspiration by the Holy Spirit. After mentioning a more excellent way, he did not transition to a new subject but expanded the thought by informing the Corinthians that their spirituality amounted to very little without the proper foundation and motivation. Paul's "more excellent way" was to make sure that every leadership model, decision, vision, and behavior had the thread of love woven throughout (1 Cor. 13, the love chapter).

It sounds too simple, too easy, too predictable, but the further church leaders remove themselves from a love-based motivation, the more unlike Christ they will become. First John 4:8 says, "He who does not love does not know God, for God is love." Failure to lead with love disqualifies our identity with God. A leader who acts independently of the love of God is acting as if they don't know God.

As God began to reveal himself to Moses and the children of Israel, one of the first things he spoke to them was the Ten Commandments. They were, in effect, the top ten ways to please him. A violation of any of God's top ten would invite, if not incite, his disapproval, which in turn would usher in consequences. On the surface, these commandments appear austere. After all, who wants to live their life under the legalistic code of "Thou shalt not"?

However, as God began unpacking his expectations of Israel in their part of keeping covenant with him, he tucked in a principle, saying he would "[show] mercy to thousands, to those who love Me and keep My commandments" (Exod. 20:6). Did you catch it? His covenant does not work in the absence of love-inspired actions.

If you have the first two commandments right, all the others will fall into place. If you love God with all your heart, soul, and mind, and love your neighbor as yourself (Matthew 22:37-39 KJV), then all the other commandments will naturally follow. If you love God, as a rule, you will not lie, steal, commit adultery, or any of the other "thou shalt nots." It's sort of like buttoning your shirt or blouse in the morning: if you get the first button in the first button-hole, all the other buttons will naturally button the way the designer intended. If you misalign the first button, none of the others will line up properly, and you'll embarrass yourself.

Jesus refreshed this theme in John 15:14 (TLB): "You are my friends if you obey me." Obedience is hard to hear and even harder to do, but no covenant exists without expectations placed upon those committed to it. If we love Jesus, we will obey him, plain and simple. If we do not obey him, then it is assumed we do not love him. Fortunately, God never commands or demands anything of those who love him that is not for their own good. Obeying God and his word is the best way for any human being to live.

A newly purchased car comes with an owner's manual. I'm sure very few new owners take the time to sit down with a cup of coffee and read that manual cover to cover. Contained in that manual are the manufacturer's recommendations for optimum operation of the vehicle they created. Owners can toss the manual, ignore the manufacturer's recommendations, and decide they are going to operate the vehicle their way. But let's see how well the vehicle performs and how long it lasts under that plan. One of our church bus drivers filled the

[handwritten margin notes: "Jesus said unto him, thou shalt love the Lord thy God with all thy heart, and with all thy soul, and with all thy mind. This is the first and great commandment. And the second is like unto you, thou shalt love thy neighbor as thyself"]

tank with diesel instead of gas. The bus made it out of the gas station but not much further. It was an expensive lesson.

Any time one of God's laws is broken, consequences will follow. People who decide they want to be promiscuous run the risk of being afflicted with an STD. But those who honor God's plan and live in a monogamous heterosexual marriage relationship run no such risk. I heard about a pastor of a large church in a Scandinavian country who was visiting India on a mission. He was standing on the second-floor balcony of his hotel overlooking the parking lot. The property was under renovation and, there was no barrier at the end of the balcony. He told the local pastor he had so much faith that he was going to step off the balcony, and God would empower him to walk on air. He disregarded the fact that God also created gravity (as well as common sense), and the pastor ended up in the emergency room with a broken leg.

Paul said that a successful walk with God boils down to three things: faith, hope, and love. Faith qualifies and hope energizes, but love mobilizes! Leading in the kingdom of God does not work without the inspirational root of love. There can be vision, action, and results, but if love is not the motivation the product will not be fully formed into the image of Christ.

Jesus is the goal of all theology, all ministry, all discipleship, and all leadership. If it isn't about Jesus, it isn't about anything. Our supreme example is the only unflawed leader of all history. To follow him is to do all things well, to follow something else is illegal, irresponsible, and injures the body of Christ.

CHAPTER 2

CHRISTLIKE LEADERS FOLLOW HIS STEPS

For to this you were called, because Christ also suffered for us, leaving us an example, that you should follow His steps (1 Pet. 2:21).

"A leader is one who knows the way, goes the way and shows the way."—John Maxwell

Could Jesus lead a twenty-first-century congregation? Of course, he could. But what would it look like? It is interesting to examine all that the church has become two thousand years after Jesus founded it. I sometimes wonder if Jesus would recognize what he started. Alexander Graham Bell invented the telephone, but I doubt he saw the smartphone coming. Henry Ford envisioned the modern automobile, but he undoubtedly would be astounded by the models parked on Ford showroom floors today.

What would a local church look like today if Jesus were the pastor? Would it have a building? How many would the sanctuary seat? Would the building be paid for? Would people sing from hymnals or LED screens? Would they sit in pews or chairs? How would they conduct worship and offerings? Would they have a gym or fellowship hall? How high would the platform be, and what would be the style of the pulpit? Would they have an outreach department? Would Jesus ever be invited to speak beyond the walls of his local church? Would he buy his clothes off the rack or have them tailored? What kind of car would he drive?

Of course, no one knows the precise answers to any of these questions, but perhaps pondering them will help us think about making room for the first-century Jesus in the context of our own lives. I am interested in discovering the answers to the following questions: What kind of a leader was Jesus? What attitude did his leadership team possess? What was the nature of the culture Jesus created among his closest followers? I believe we can at least approach the answers to some of these questions.

Jesus Christ would have to be in the conversation as the greatest leader of all time. For example, historian and nonbeliever H. G. Wells said, "I must confess as a historian that this penniless preacher from Nazareth is irrevocably the very center of history. Jesus Christ is easily the most dominant figure of all history." When John Ortberg was asked why he traveled the country teaching about the greatness of the leadership of Jesus, he responded, "Who would you believe would last longer, the powerful Roman Empire, or a little Jewish rabbi with twelve inexperienced followers?" He punctuated his answer with, "We are still naming our children Matthew, James, Sarah and Mary, and we call our dogs Nero and Caesar."[1]

Jesus didn't write books, he didn't graduate from a university, he didn't conduct seminars for large gatherings, he didn't have a catchy slogan or boast of celebrated followers. He didn't develop a music ministry, draft a creative team, train a drama group, or establish an outreach department. He didn't ride in a fancy chariot, maintain a suite of offices, or wait around to sign autographs after performing miracles. He didn't do any of the things that typically accompany greatness and success; he simply invested his daily life in the twelve men who became his fully devoted followers called "disciples." After

---

[1]   Ken Blanchard, Phil Hodges, et al., *Lead Like Jesus* (Nashville, TN: Thomas Nelson, 2016).

only forty-two months of training, he entrusted his vision and mission to them.

Typically, we don't think about Jesus as a leader. Instead, we think about him theologically as Son of God, Son of Man, High Priest, Messiah, Savior, or Lord. We eagerly emphasize his compassion toward the hurting. His supernatural ministry dominates the Gospel texts and reveals his unique class as both God and man. But these descriptors do not encompass all that Jesus was.

Jesus was the ultimate leader. The movement he initiated two millenniums ago is still alive and thriving. It still maintains his original values, message, and mission, and has a presence in most every nation and territory of the world. No other leader who has stepped on the world's stage can boast of such an enduring impact. Of course, we recognize that Jesus founded more than a mere enterprise; it is the continuously operating, ever-expanding spiritual body Jesus branded as "My church" (Matt. 16:18). *And I say also unto thee, that*

Jesus identified the gates of hell as the most formidable foe in *thou art* the building of his church, but he was quick to declare that even hell's *Peter,* resistance would not prevent the advancement of the mission of his *and upon this rock* church. We understand the supernatural power of Christ resident *I will* within the church, but there is something more: one of the reasons *build my* for the great advancement of the church is the Christlike leadership *church;* that God raises up to lead his people forward into great victory and *and the gates of* kingdom expansion. *hell shall*

The culture, condition, and location of every local church is *not pre-* the result of leadership—nothing more, nothing less. Churches will *vail* either grow and advance in their community or dwindle and close *against* because of one thing: leadership. No local church wins the growth-*it.* and-revival lottery. God doesn't love one congregation more than another. John Maxwell's mantra says it all: "Everything rises and falls with leadership."

Everything about a local church is a direct reflection of the one who is leading it, including the vision, attitude, size, and quality. In rare situations congregations suffer and decline because of oppressed economies or natural disasters. When crisis comes, however, called leaders respond and find ways to recover and perhaps rebound stronger than before. Intuitive leaders are comfortable leading in chaotic times. Uncertainty about the future provides job security for such leaders.

An office manager or basketball coach can choose any leadership model they desire. A church leader, however, has no other option but to study and imitate Jesus as a leadership model. Every church leader has been called by God to be a shepherd who follows the model of Jesus. First Peter 2:21 says, "You should follow His steps." Jeremiah 3:15 (NLT) says, "I will give you shepherds after my own heart, who will guide you with knowledge and understanding."

Psalm 78:70–72 says, "He also chose David His servant, and took him from the sheepfolds; from following the ewes that had young He brought him, to shepherd Jacob His people, and Israel His inheritance. So he shepherded them according to the integrity of his heart, and guided them by the skillfulness of his hands."

David developed his leadership style and people skills while tending his father's sheep. These skills, derived from the overflow of his great heart for God, are what attracted God's attention and qualified him for promotion as Israel's next king. Christlike leaders develop their heart for God and his people long before they occupy a leadership role. (Take a lesson from David: if you've got it when no one is looking, you will have a better chance of doing well when everyone is looking.)

While attending Bible college, I drove a special-needs bus route for a public school. I had never been around physically or mentally challenged children, so my learning curve was huge. Eventually I learned to care for and love them unconditionally. I drove these kids back and forth to school every day for two years. I got to know their families and occasionally would spend time after hours with them. They taught me the virtues of patience, compassion, thankfulness, and tolerance. As clueless as I was on the day I got the job, I sincerely believe that time with these special children helped prepare me for my pastoral future. Incidentally, I'm not ashamed to admit that after I dropped the last child off on my last day of work, I wept all the way back to the bus terminal. I was changed forever.

Jesus was presented with every pastoral and leadership issue imaginable: rebellion, adultery, demonic possession, family dysfunction, mistreatment of children, betrayal from a staff member, personal mistreatment, and growth problems. Once he was appreciated by only 10 percent of those whose lives he changed (e.g., only one cleansed leper returned to give thanks). He was misunderstood by family members and lied about. His motives were misjudged, his words misinterpreted, his values misrepresented by staff members. A close relative/preacher/mentor was arrested and executed. People walked out while he was preaching. He fed the hungry on a shoe-string budget. He had big letdowns after big-event days. He was highly spoken of on a Sunday, but by Thursday some of the same people wanted him dead. His greatest act was doubted by a close follower, and his most highly trained staff members were paralyzed with fear. His designated spokesman lied, cried, and denied him.

It doesn't take many years for a pastor or a church leader to see just about everything under the sun. In forty-two months, Jesus confronted nearly every aspect of pastoring, faced every decision leaders face, and dealt with all kinds of personalities and agendas. But we should underscore the fact that Jesus never had a meltdown, never lost his cool, never surrendered his credibility by violating confidentiality, never prayed publicly about other people's personal problems, never brought his anger to the pulpit, never mistreated little people, never emotionally engaged a woman or met with one alone behind closed doors, never mismanaged money or manipulated his followers, never changed his theology because of a moral compromise in his life, and never made leadership decisions that situated life easier for himself at the expense of making life more cumbersome for his followers.

It was said of Jesus that he did "all things well" (Mark 7:37). There is no aspect of Jesus's leadership model that any church leader today can look at and say, "Well that was stupid" or "I would never do that" or "That was kind of shady." Regrettably, some leaders, as well as church members, act like they have a better idea than Jesus about how his church should be led. They don't want Jesus standing in the way while they run his business.

And were beyond measure astonished, saying, he hath done 29 all things well: he maketh both the deaf to hear, and the dumb to speak.

Many years ago, a popular acronym in commercial Christianity was "WWJD" (What Would Jesus Do?). It was printed on coffee cups, wristbands, T-shirts, Bible covers, and bumper stickers and even tattooed. I'm sure it generated a handsome sum for the creator, but it's doubtful that it made an impact on anyone's behavior. Through the years, WWJD has become somewhat cheesy, but it is undoubtedly a great question. I have tried to look through Jesus's eyes on numerous occasions, and it has helped considerably.

Undeniably, many church leaders have miserably failed in doing what Jesus would have done. Perhaps they should have asked themselves the question: What would Jesus *not* do?" But on the other side of the pulpit, I'm not sure how well some twenty-first-century church members would do in a congregation pastored by Jesus. Perhaps he would place too much emphasis on sacrifice or say offensive things like, "If you want to be in this church, you must take up your cross and follow me." He might require his leadership team to stop hiding behind their ministry and actually go on his mission and make disciples. Perhaps he would stand near the offering basket and watch what people gave—then use it as a teaching point. He might call out hypocrites and critics, and instead of answering their accusations, he might have a few probing questions of his own!

When I was twenty-five, I was unanimously elected pastor of a small family-owned-and-operated congregation. To my grief, I soon found out that my initial popularity was unsustainable. Jesus may have got elected there, but I somehow doubt his popularity would have lasted very long either. And if *he* couldn't survive there, what hope did I have?

For one thing, there was no designated pastor's office in the church. The rationale was the church board didn't want me to have an on-campus office because I might want a "high-back leather chair behind my desk to impress my friends." One Sunday morning when I introduced my wife's uncle as our guest speaker, there was only a weak welcoming applause. Later I asked a man about it, and he answered piously, "We wouldn't want him to get a big head now, would we?" Not only were they protecting my preacher relatives from getting a big head, they also were careful not to fatten up their wallets. They didn't want me giving offerings to any of them when they came to preach. "If you asked them to come over and fix your sink," they reasoned, "you wouldn't pay them, would you?"

They thought I had espoused false doctrine because I taught sinners Bible studies in their homes, where they repented and came to church ready to be baptized. They reasoned that since no one in the congregation had seen these sinners repent, they *couldn't* be ready to be baptized. One board member thumped his finger in my chest and questioned if I was called to preach. His friend chimed in with the comment, "You don't have a real job."

They insisted my job was to take care of the "spiritual" aspect of the church, and they would oversee the "temporal." I responded by pointing out that the apostle Peter had instructed me to "take the oversight" of the church and explained that financial stewardship was theological and therefore spiritual. (See Luke 16:11.) Still, one board member pulled me aside to explain their congregational theology, insisting it was not my place to look at his or anyone else's steward-ship record. I thought, *What are you hiding?* but I said, "Well then, I don't think you would have wanted Jesus to be your pastor."

[handwritten margin note: If therefore ye have not been faithful in the unrighteous mammon, who will commit to your trust the true riches.]

He said, "What do you mean by that?"

"Well, Jesus stood near the offertory and watched what people gave. If he did it, he had a good reason, and I think I know what the reason is. A pastor needs to know if people are faithful because their giving record demonstrates whether or not they are in financial cov-enant with God and qualified to lead in the church."

He stammered and sputtered and finally uttered, "Well… Jesus may have done it, but, but…you can't!"

I said, "Well, I just want to be like Jesus." He shook his head and walked off. I'm afraid Jesus would have a hard time getting elected in some places today.

I learned a powerful lesson on the golf course one day. I enjoy playing golf. After all, it is holey ground. I was introduced to the game by two men in a church where I served as youth pastor. They bought me a used set of clubs for my birthday, and then took me out on the course to acquaint me with the game. Like most golfers, I learned many things on my own that, unfortunately, were incorrect.

I soon began scoring consistently in the mid-eighties, but decided I wanted to improve, so I bought a lesson with a pro.

The golf pro took me out to the driving range and asked me to hit a shot with my seven iron. I was a little intimidated to say the least, but I obediently pulled the seven iron from my bag and addressed the ball. Before I even swung the club, he cried, "*Stop!* Why did you do that?"

"Do what?" I asked. I didn't think I had done anything yet.

"Why did you address the ball with only your left hand on the club?"

"Well, it feels comfortable, and I've seen other golfers do it."

He said, "Have you ever watched professional golfers?"

I had been given a one-day pass to a professional golf tournament about three years prior, so I said yes. Then he rocked my world: "Have you ever seen a golf pro address the ball with only one hand on the club?"

"Well, no."

"Then why are *you* doing it?" (That will be fifty dollars please!)

I get that, but I do not get church leaders who continually do things Jesus would never have done. Of course, there will only be one Jesus, but he did tell his disciples, "The things that I am doing, you are going to do." (See John 14:12.) Paul said, "Imitate me as I imitate Christ" (1 Cor. 11:1, GW). Peter and John were criticized for acting just like Jesus (Acts 4:13). It took them a while to get there, but they finally made it. Could we be so fortunate to be guilty of the same?

Jesus is the goal of all leadership in his church. Study Jesus (Matt. 11:29), fellowship Jesus (Phil. 3:10), walk with Jesus (Luke 24:15), follow Jesus (Matt. 9:9), and imitate Jesus (John 14:12). If Jesus did it, you do it! If Jesus didn't do it, don't you do it! Peter perhaps said it best: "For to this you were called, because Christ also suffered for us, leaving us an example, that you should follow His steps" (1 Pet. 2:21).

CHAPTER 3

CHRISTLIKE LEADERS KNOW HIS VOICE

And when he brings out his own sheep, he goes before them; and the sheep follow him, for they know his voice.

Yet they will by no means follow a stranger, but will flee from him, for they do not know the voice of strangers (John 10:4–5).

"If we don't know where we're going, we might end up somewhere else."—Yogi Berra

The greatest book on leadership ever written is the Bible. Great leaders and speakers who expound on the subject today are expressing what scripture has taught for millenniums. Oswald Sanders wrote, "Leadership is influence."[2] John Maxwell taught that everything rises and falls on leadership.[3] The greatest mark of a leader is not what they established while on earth, but what happens to

---

[2] Oswald Sanders, *Spiritual Leadership* (Chicago, IL: Moody Publishers, 1967, 1980, 1994, 2007).
[3] John Maxwell, *The Success Journey* (Nashville: Thomas Nelson, 1997).

their life's work after they're gone. Will it go to a new level, or will it go to the grave with them?

Jesus could not boast of millions or even thousands of followers the day he launched his church. In fact, you could argue that his best efforts largely appeared to fail. On two occasions, several thousand disciples gathered to eat loaves and fishes. Paul testified that Jesus was seen by five hundred at one time after his resurrection (perhaps at his ascension). However, just a few days later there were only 120 who yet remained in the upper room, faithfully waiting for the promise of the Father. In less than two weeks, the number of his official followers dropped 76 percent!

Perhaps the greatest indicator of Jesus's credibility was the fact that his first followers laid down their lives for him. Some would argue that followers of cult leaders have done the same, but they typically perish in acts of suicide or various death-wish scenarios. The leaders Jesus trained were so passionate about his mission, so effective in delivering it to the world, and so willing to die for him that they gladly lined up to lay down their lives. Of course, they had been eyewitnesses of his great sacrifice on the cross and of the resurrection. Josh McDowell declared that Jesus was either liar, lunatic, or Lord.[4] The way the disciples died confirms that Jesus was an authentic leader and his mission was worthy of their ultimate sacrifice.

The Roman Empire tried to crush Christ's work, but after the empire fell, Jesus and his church were still standing. The movement that he birthed two thousand years ago is not only alive, but today is advancing in nearly every nation and territory of the world. Undoubtedly, we understand that the resurrection of Jesus Christ changed everything, and we affirm that the gift of salvation is a powerful force. But without his model of leadership, without his training and disciple-making of the future leaders of the church, and without the greatest leadership book ever written (the Bible), the church would hardly have endured beyond the first century.

---

[4] Josh McDowell, *Evidence That Demands a Verdict* (Nashville, TN: Thomas Nelson, 2017).

Jesus put something into the twelve that had both immediate and residual impact on each of them. Not only did the miracles impress them, but so did the way he spoke to the sick. Not only did his authority over demons amaze them, but his aftercare for the delivered was equally impressive. Not only did the size of the crowds captivate them, but their greatest moments with him occurred after the multitude was gone and they were at last alone with their teacher.

Jesus's lens of love, acceptance, respect, and forgiveness was quite an adjustment from the pharisaical optic of judgment, politics, insensitivity, skepticism, violence, dishonesty, betrayal, and murder. He had work to do in reprogramming the leadership outlook of his disciples. How gifted of a leader would it take to rescue them from their mediocrity? Could he successfully deprogram the disciples' broken leadership model? What strategy would he employ? How long did he have to get it done?

While the disciples were peering through the leadership lens of their religious realities, Jesus was offering a radically different view. James and John (and their mother) jockeyed early and often for position. Peter was a man of action and willing to lead, but he seemed to open his mouth only to change feet. He also was quick to draw his sword at the first sign of a threat. (Luckily for his victim, he was unskilled). Nathaniel was initially skeptical of the reputation of Jesus's hometown, a place of no consequence, and judged him accordingly. Simon the Zealot carried a concealed dagger, having sworn to take out any Roman authorities or military personnel when the opportunity presented itself. Matthew was collecting taxes for the government that was hated by those Jesus was trying to reach. How is that for a marketing strategy? Judas never did subscribe to Jesus's mission and eventually became Satan's accomplice in attempting to defeat it.

Much of Jesus's teaching was a pushback against the religious hierarchy whose policies further empowered the powerful and penalized the powerless. Jesus characterized the natures of some of these religious leaders as vipers, devourers, hypocrites, glory-seekers, blind guides, void of justice, unmerciful, faithless, majoring on minors, lawless, mausoleums, sons of those who murdered Israel's prophets.

Jesus's biggest problem with the religious leaders, however, was that their mouths were writing checks that their actions could not cash. Sound familiar? We've all seen it as Jesus saw it. The religious brain trust could not perform the behaviors they demanded of their subjects; they required more from them than they did from themselves. When leaders demand more from their followers than they do from themselves, they are not following Jesus.

Not so from the leadership team Jesus built, although their initial efforts were unimpressive. One might think Jesus should have selected disciples from the hallowed halls of universities or from the Who's Who of first-century Judea. Laurie Beth Jones speculates that he might have hoped his disciples smelled more like heavenly phosphoresce and less like mud and dead fish.[5] And yet this ragtag bunch of nondescript laborers distinguished themselves by changing the world and ultimately having their names inscribed on the twelve foundations of the New Jerusalem (Rev. 21:14).

Ancient rabbis traversed the dusty hillsides of Judea with their eager disciples in tow. It was said that disciples were collecting the dust from their master's feet. Is your life of leadership gathering dust from the feet of Rabbi Jesus? I know you've obeyed his gospel. I know you have been called to lead. I know you have a prayer life, and I know you love Jesus. But are you leading others as you follow in his steps, or are you following something else?

Not everyone who has been saved by Jesus Christ is living in obedience to him. This shouldn't be a surprise. Many who claim Christianity as their ideology manifest attitudes and behaviors that are from a zip code far from where Jesus lived. Peter preached that "God has made that same Jesus...both Lord and Christ" (Acts 2:36). Everybody wants a Savior, but who wants a master? Everybody wants their sin problem remedied by Messiah, but who wants a Lord telling him/her what to do?

Is every called leader in the kingdom of God living in strict obedience to the one who called them? If so, we would have no unhealthy leaders or congregations. Jesus said, "If you love me, keep

---

[5] Laurie Beth Jones, *Jesus CEO* (New York, NY: Hyperion, 1995).

my commandments (John 14:15). Another translation says, "If you love me, *obey me*" (TLB, emphasis mine). Wouldn't you agree the second wording is a bit stronger? Jesus proved his love for us on the cross, but how do we prove our love for him? There is no other way to demonstrate our love for Jesus except through a faithful obedience to his commands and his model of leadership.

Church leaders are stewards of the human resources God had placed in their hands. The subject of stewardship reaches far beyond the parameters of finances. Stewardship is about how we manage *everything* God has placed in our hands, not just our money. God is the owner of everything (Ps. 24:1), and we are his managers. A manager's job is to fulfill the wishes of his or her employer.

One Sunday morning I introduced the subject of stewardship by asking if anyone in the audience had a one-hundred-dollar bill. A man on the front row raised his hand. "Please give it to me," I asked. He stood up, reached into his pocket, and gave it to me without question. I took it, placed it in my pocket, walked away, and continued my message.

I quickly noted that some in the audience were a little perturbed at me for taking his money without any explanation or even saying "thanks." I finally asked the congregation, "Are you upset with me for taking this man's money? What you don't know is that I gave him that one-hundred-dollar bill before the service and asked him to keep it for me. You were upset with me for demanding that he give me that one-hundred-dollar bill, but the man knew it was mine and was simply being a good steward of my money. He did exactly what I told him to do with it.

Church leaders are not to be lords over God's heritage. The congregations or ministries we lead are not ours. In fact, I am careful to never refer to the people that I pastor as "my church." I've lived by this conviction for many years. In fact, I wince a little bit when I hear another pastor say it. At best, a local pastor is an "undershepherd" serving the "great Shepherd" (Hebrews 13:20). Our local churches are not ours to own and operate but rather they belong to the founder of the church, Jesus Christ. Our job is to steward the church under his authority and direction.

The Pharisees practiced selective stewardship, namely, the financial aspect of stewardship. They even tithed on the spices in their cabinet. But when it came to the stewardship of the people in their communities, they were abysmal failures. Their modeling was a sham, their legalistic soteriology placed well-intentioned proselytes in double jeopardy, and woe to the helpless widow under their purview.

Stewardship cannot be compartmentalized or limited to the financial aspect of our lives. Stewardship is holistic in that it touches every moving part of our lives. Our bank accounts and our calendars are theological documents, revealing whether or not we practice what we preach. A quick printout of a single page of either our operations account or our planner will quickly reveal whether or not we are in obedience to God and qualified to lead others. Church leaders must lead in the stead of Jesus Christ, and we must take heed how he wants us to steward ourselves as well as those we lead.

I once attended a ministers' business meeting where a resolution was introduced that, in my estimation, was legalistic and judgmental. It seemed to create a sort of thought police that assumed treachery rather than trust among ministers. I was young, new to the area, and had no position, prestige, or influence. However, there was something about the spirit of this legislation that immediately grieved my spirit. After the reading of and motions to adopt the resolution, there were many favorable comments from the floor, but absolutely no debate. In an unprecedented action, the superintendent vacated the chair to come down to the floor and advocated for the resolution. He mentioned that he would be proud for this policy to come to the national organization from our conference. The vote was going to be a slam dunk.

The voters began to call for the question. The next thing I knew, I was standing and calling for the floor. When the vice chair recognized me, I said words to this effect: "Mr. Vice Chairman, with all due respect, we are about to initiate something we may regret in years to come. In the preamble, we are informed that there are 'wolves in sheep's clothing' among us, and we are assured this policy will eliminate that alleged problem. I've traveled this country a little bit, and I can't tell who these 'wolves' are. But Jesus told us in Matthew 18 how to address issues like this. He didn't advocate for legislation, but rather prescribed the approach of using the capital of relationship and going to them alone and restoring them. I submit that there's no provision for what Jesus told us to do in this policy."

I continued, "If we're trying to upgrade the spiritual level of our constituency, then I offer an amendment requiring every minister to fast two days a week and pray one hour a day. But if we are truly desiring complete transparency among us, then I offer another amendment requiring every pastor to bring their church financial records annually to this conference for accountability." I concluded, "Instead of being proud, I would be ashamed for this policy to come to the national organization from us." It was unanimously voted down. Jesus's leadership model and words should always get the vote in his church.

Dale Carnegie said, "The man who starts out going nowhere, generally gets there." There is a temptation for leaders in the church to stray from the footsteps of the one who called, anointed, and chose them. Following Jesus often departs from the path we want to travel. If you are following in his steps, you will pass the mile markers named humility, selflessness, and servanthood. Leaders who are truly called must continually make corrections, recalibrate direction, and return to the footsteps of Jesus. Tragically, once some leaders receive their paperwork to lead, they gradually veer over to a path that only vaguely resembles the steps of Jesus, if at all.

Jesus said that one day many would claim him, identify with him, and understand the authority of his name. He said they would use his name to perform great miracles, declare prophecies, and even cast out devils. But Jesus also said that eventually he would have to tell them, "I never knew you. Get away from me, you who break God's laws" (Matt. 7:21–23, NLT). This is a stunning revelation, especially knowing that Jesus commanded all believers to go and demonstrate these very signs in his name (Mark 16).

Who are these people? What laws of God did they break? These people were not pagans or heathens. They obviously understood principles of faith and the power in the name of Jesus. We can assume they wore some label of Christianity. But whatever laws Jesus was citing were obviously not in their operator's manual. If the Bible is its own best interpreter, and if we remain in the context of Jesus's comments about these believers who broke God's law, then the answer must be found in his Mount Olivet discourse of Matthew 5–7.

These three chapters seem to be the central corpus of Jesus's teaching and mission. There appears to be one continuous theme in this passage rather than three unrelated ideas. In chapter 5, a great multitude is following him, but he calls the twelve in close and delivers his message primarily to them. Almost every concept Jesus presented in the ensuing Beatitudes contradicted the "best practices" of the contemporary religious culture. Pious leaders of that day knew nothing about being poor in spirit, mourning, meekness, hungering and thirsting for righteousness, mercy, purity of heart, making peace, or being persecuted.

But Jesus didn't stop there. He said that if the righteousness of his followers did not exceed the righteousness of the teachers of religious law and that of the Pharisees, they would never enter the kingdom of heaven (Matt. 5:20). Everything under law was superseded by grace. Jesus's law says that adultery and murder can now be committed in the heart. He taught that an appearance at an altar of sacrificial worship cannot be blessed without first having one's relationships set aright. He advised that frivolous divorces and vows are not permissible. He exposed them to the laws of turning the other cheek, going the second mile, yielding to a borrower's request, and loving one's enemies. The Pharisees practiced none of these things and showed no remorse.

That was only chapter 5. In chapter 6, Jesus shared secrets of pleasing God: the Lord's Prayer model, how to fast effectively, how to lay up treasure in heaven, how to be filled with darkness or light, serving God or money, and living an anxiety-free life. In chapter 7, he confronted judgmental attitudes, how to ask, seek, and knock, how to walk the narrow way, and how people are identified by the fruit they bear. Keep in mind that this entire discourse was designed to reset the polluted piety of the Pharisees, indicating they represented the opposite of everything about God's new law that Jesus had just revealed.

Now we arrive at the shocking moment when Jesus declared he didn't know certain people who assumed their good standing with him and their access into eternity with him. What was the basis of Christ's rejection of them? Did these people spend more time practicing the supernatural than manifesting God's law? Were they rejected at the door of eternity for being mighty in the Holy Spirit but void of intimacy with Jesus? Did they have power without position, miracles without manifestation, faith without fruit, and testimonies but no testament? Jesus didn't know them.

We typically identify these who were rejected by Jesus as quasi believers who found cover somewhere under the canopy of Christianity but who did not have relationship with Jesus. It's impossible to have a relationship with him without first obeying his gospel, yet there are those who have obeyed his gospel and still haven't developed relationship with him. Is there a category of Christians who have obeyed his gospel but not him? Apparently so!

The ultimate test at the door of heaven is relationship. Anyone in a vibrant relationship with Jesus Christ is sure to obey him and therefore be identified as his. Those intimately engaged with Jesus Christ are sure to reflect his attitude, values, and priorities. Paul said, "You must have the same attitude that Christ Jesus had (Phil. 2:5, NLT).

The writer of Hebrews refers us to "the doctrine of Christ" (6:1). Is it possible to know the doctrine of Jesus but not practice the attitude of Jesus? Perhaps this is a way to better understand that "the letter kills, but the Spirit gives life" (2 Cor. 3:6). Is it possible to follow Jesus from such a great distance that we are collecting no dust from the rabbi's feet? Paul said, "If anyone does not have the Spirit of Christ, he is not His" (Rom. 8:9).

For every strength there is a weakness. Some faith traditions emphasize the supernatural move of the Holy Spirit. That would be me because I'm Pentecostal. Pentecostals believe every problem can be solved in one good altar service. To be sure, a good visitation of God during an altar service can improve many situations, but perhaps our weakness is that we have majored on the power of Jesus and minored on the person of Jesus.

Perhaps the power and the person of Jesus are synthesized in Jesus's invitation found in Matthew 11:29 (KJV): "Learn of me." Learn the orthodoxy of Jesus, then follow the orthopraxy of Jesus.

That is how Jesus conducted business. Luke recalled this method when he wrote, "The former account I made...of all that Jesus began both to do and teach" (Acts 1:1). Jesus did something, then he unpacked what he had done to train his followers, then they did it. This method of training leaders not only gave them the doctrine of Jesus, but also the attitude of Jesus.

Many Christian leaders believe they are walking with Jesus Christ as did his disciples. But occasionally life experiences reveal their blind spots, and the exposure can be eye-opening, if not disappointing. Have you ever been surprised by the words coming out of your mouth? Have you ever presented an attitude toward someone that you later regretted? One would think that spending quality time with Jesus every day would quickly reveal his method of operation to the disciples (as well as we). However, James and John were upset with the Samaritans for rejecting Jesus's ministry. These two disciples felt assured that when they asked Jesus for permission to blast Samaria with fire and brimstone that he would promptly give his blessing. Instead, they received a rebuke and then a revelation of what had motivated their rogue response.

Jesus responded, "You do not know what manner of spirit you are of. For the Son of Man did not come to destroy men's lives but to save them" (Luke 9:55). The word *spirit* was not a reference to the Holy Spirit but rather to their human spirit, which was perhaps operating under the influence of a cultural prejudice against the Samaritans. Anytime a leader's words, actions, or behavior cripples, maims, or injures, they are not operating under the Spirit of Jesus Christ. They may be following in someone's steps, but certainly not the steps of Rabbi Jesus.

Unhealthy people enjoy confrontation. Leaders with the attitude of Christ, however, will avoid unnecessary confrontation with the understanding that at some point it may become necessary. At such a time, they will use Jesus's prescription in Matthew 18. Most issues can be handled, as Jesus said, "alone."

Years ago, in an Injoy Life Club leadership lesson, John Maxwell addressed the subject "Confrontation, the Thing Nobody Wants to Do." I have used this many times and have taught it to my leaders:

1. Meet the person alone.
2. Affirm your love for them and recognize something positive in their life.
3. Tell them what your issue is.
4. Let them know how you feel about what they did or said.
5. Let them respond to your concern.
6. Repeat back to them in your words what you think they just said, so there is no confusion.
7. Suggest positive options moving forward.
8. Bring the meeting to a redemptive conclusion.

Unhealthy people enjoy confrontation and are quick to engage it. They like the buzz that comes by releasing their pent-up frustration upon those they perceive are under their control. Unhealthy church leaders will brag to their colleagues about how they confronted people, running them off, blowing them up, or straightening them out. But if redemption is not the goal of confrontation, then Christ is not in the room.

This should be a warning for church leaders who place high demands on their followers but do not hold themselves to the same standard of accountability. Church leaders who demand prayer, fasting, worship, and sacrificial giving of their followers without praying, fasting, worshipping, or giving sacrificially themselves are nothing more than modern Pharisees. They give themselves a pass, overestimating their status with God while penalizing patrons who chronically fail to measure up to their standard, which ironically falls short of the real goal. Where this dynamic is present, there are sure to be high levels of arrogance and corruption among the leaders and low levels of morale and trust among the followers.

Jesus said, "Learn of me" and "know my voice."

CHAPTER 4

CHRISTLIKE LEADERS HAVE CHRISTLIKE MENTORS

Then He went down with them…to Nazareth, and was subject to them, but His mother kept all these things in her heart. And Jesus increased in wisdom and stature, and in favor with God and men (Luke 2:51–52).

"A big man is one who makes us feel bigger when we are with him."—Unknown

Jesus was a man in every way any man is a man. His mind developed, his body grew, and his flesh was tempted. He experienced childhood, puberty, adolescence, and adulthood. There was nothing unusual about his flesh, except that he was the image of the invisible God. He had siblings, cousins, aunts, uncles, grandparents, friends and elders in the community, and rabbis. No doubt he experienced bumps and bruises as a little boy, and as a man he worked hard at his trade. His mind and body functioned like any other man, experiencing hunger, exhaustion, exhilaration, discouragement, questions, anticipation, temptation, and approval.

Jesus did not live in a divine vacuum, unaffected by family, culture, or community. He was impacted, at least in some measure, by formative influences. Of course, none of these external influences proved detrimental to the fulfillment of his mission. However, he did develop views, values, personality, mannerisms, speech patterns, style of presentation, all of which were gathered and revealed perhaps like fingerprints on his life.

At age twelve Jesus demonstrated superior understanding of the scriptures as he captivated the resident temple doctors of the law. But when confronted by his parents, instead of reacting with arrogance and condescension (as would many novices with special giftings), instead of being embarrassed by their protestations of concern, he subjected himself to their correction. Consequently, he "increased in wisdom and stature, and in favor with God and men."

Given these influences, scripture is clear that he neither spoke like the scribes (Matt. 7:29) nor acted like the Pharisees nor followed the accepted teaching pattern of other rabbis. In short, he did not behave like a typical first-century male. I love this about Jesus. Why be predictable, boring, and disappointing? Jesus had a magnetic personality. He noticed people, he spoke to people, and he was kind to people. He was not annoying or obnoxious. Even children were drawn to him.

There can be no question concerning Mary and Joseph's impact upon his early life. Jesus was not immune to the oversight, love, care, concern, instruction, and the modeling of his parents. Another early influencer perhaps was his older cousin John. In my book *Follow to Lead,*[6] I suggested that John the Baptist prepared the way for Jesus in more ways than one: "There are several similar patterns in their overlapping ministries. John and Jesus both came out of the wilderness to launch their ministries." They both made disciples who outlived their rabbis and imitated them until they died—except that many

---

[6] Stan O. Gleason, *Follow to Lead: The Journey of a Disciple Maker* (Weldon Spring, MO: Word Aflame Press, 2016), 68.

years later John's disciples at Ephesus received further theological enlightenment from Paul (Acts 19:1–6). Rabbis did not commonly baptize their disciples, but John and Jesus baptized theirs. It was the privilege of every rabbi to introduce his disciples to the world, as did John at Jesus's baptism, and as did the Spirit of Jesus on the Day of Pentecost (John 14:17-18).

John Donne wrote, "No man is an island…every man is a piece of the continent, a part of the main." Jesus could not have impacted the world from afar. He was embedded in the very culture and society he was trying to reach. He became one of us and therefore subjected himself to the human influences around him. How much did they impact him? You decide.

Ralph Waldo Emerson said, "The mind, once stretched by a new idea, never returns to its original dimensions." The apostle Paul expressed it spiritually: "Be transformed by the renewing of your mind, that you may prove what is that good and acceptable and perfect will of God" (Rom. 12:2). We understand from scripture that all of life is first lived in the mind. Proverbs says, "As a man thinks in his heart, so he is."

The way we think has been shaped by various influential people whose mouths and lives have spoken words and formed images that are etched in our memory. Many of the things these influencers spoke have become woven into the fabric of our daily living. I've often wondered how much differently some people's lives would have unfolded had they been exposed to healthier leaders, parents, or other influencers.

I am a product of a local church as well as the church at large. Having been privileged to grow up in a Christian minister's home, I have been exposed to some of the greatest leaders, teachers, preachers, apostles, prophets, evangelists, pastors, and saints that anyone could hope for. My backyard, so to speak, was our church campus, which also shared facilities with a world-changing Bible college. My father was an instructor there for thirty-five years. It has been estimated that over half of the general board members of our national organization at a certain time were graduates of this institution. Along with other

Bible colleges and training centers, the school trained and developed leaders who have impacted the world.

One of the many dynamics I appreciated about my home church was the preaching and teaching of big ideas. My pastor(s) never wasted time majoring on minors. Only the major biblical themes were presented across the pulpit by my leaders. They often placed significant worldwide and geopolitical events within the biblical context. I knew nothing about abuses from the pulpit, such as saint-bashing, criticizing crosstown churches, the holiness clothes-line, angry preaching, control, or manipulation.

It was not a perfect culture, and like most who have grown up in the church, a few flaws did not come to light until further reflection as an adult. I thank God for my parents who created the imagery of my heroes in the church, both leaders and saints. Their emotional, mental, and spiritual well-being provided a positive perception of church leaders, the ministry, and the saints that still blesses me, my children, and grandchildren to this day.

David said, "The lines have fallen to me in pleasant places; yes, I have a good inheritance" (Ps. 16:6). He appears to be expressing appreciation for how God had situated his life for all his days. David well understood that the boundaries within which God had nurtured, prepared, and protected him were the reason he was what he was. Any called man or woman of God in their seasoned years can look back and easily see the providential hand of God directing their decisions and placing the right influencers around them. I can truly say with David that the lines have fallen to me in pleasant places, and I have a good inheritance.

Speaking through the prophet Isaiah, God said, "I have created the blacksmith who blows the coals in the fire, who brings forth an instrument for his work" (Isa. 54:16). Early in my life and ministry I was placed by God on many anvils to be forged as an instrument for his work. I am indebted to my parents, older siblings, teachers, and godly leaders who have graced and added incalculable value to my life.

There are five men especially who have helped to forge my life, beginning with my father, Wendell C. Gleason. His buoyant spirit, sterling character, and impeccable Christian model were unparalleled among his peers. One longtime colleague (of my dad) confided in me after my father's death that Dad was a "much better Christian" than he ever was. He gave his life to train the next generation of Christian leaders, but he did not do this at the cost of failing to invest in four hungry mouths that ate Cheerios at his table every morning.

I'm sure that I can speak for my older brother and two sisters when I say that perhaps his greatest accomplishment was inspiring his four children by his authentic walk with God. I will never forget rising early to go to school or work and finding him already in the corner of the family room, wrapped in a blanket on a cold, dark Minnesota morning, calling out to God. He always had a cheerful smile, an accommodating laugh, a word of high praise, a song in his heart, and a life that practiced the presence of God.

My siblings and I have often remarked that the life of our father blesses us to this day, although he's been gone twenty-three years. Perhaps the greatest lesson Dad taught me was how to forgive. I was in my early twenties and serving as assistant to the pastor at a congregation in Ohio. Someone called to let me know a great injustice had been perpetrated on this innocent man. I hurriedly packed a suitcase and raced home to defend him.

When I walked into the living room and after many hugs and tears, I said, "Dad, this isn't right. I'm going over there and straighten this whole thing out."

He protested, "Oh no, son, God is taking good care of me and I will be fine."

I persisted, "Dad, I'm going over there and giving someone a piece of my mind."

"Well, son, you know what's left if you give away too many pieces of your mind!"

"Dad, this is no time to joke around. I'm serious. I'm leaving now to confront this injustice and demand a reversal."

"No, son, I'm just praying for them."

"*Praying* for them!?" I retorted. "I can think of a few prayers I'd like to pray over them right now!" I closed my argument with "Dad, don't you think you're taking this Christianity thing a little too far?

I've never heard you say one critical thing about anyone ever, but now would be a good time. I bet you could even say something nice about the devil."

He paused, then quipped, "Well, he's a good one!" We both burst out in laughter and that was the end of the debate. That conversation was nearly forty years ago, but rehearsing it as I write it now blesses me once again. Dad took his Christianity seriously. He was always the same, never fake, ever positive, upbeat, expecting great things, hoping for the best out of everyone, and never leaving room for the devil. He taught me to follow Christ.

Perhaps the second greatest influence on my life was my first pastor, the man who dedicated me to the Lord. He also was the president of the college referenced above. Hundreds, perhaps thousands, would say that he was the greatest Bible teacher they ever heard. He had a way of explaining the complexities of scripture in laymen's terms. His preaching and teaching were brilliantly simple. He was an in-demand conference and camp-meeting speaker, but his greatest gift was teaching. I will always be indebted to him for instilling in me a love for the word of God and a desire to study and present my findings with excellence. One of his grandchildren graciously gave me one of his Bibles, which I cherish.

My first pastor's successor also played a profound role in my formative years. He was a scholar, a brilliant communicator with a powerfully persuasive personality. I would sit on the edge of my seat during his preaching. I have heard other colleagues talk about the ramblings of their pastors behind the pulpit, but I have no such story. His pulpit delivery was focused like a laser, referencing current events, engaging key biblical texts, relying on a powerful anointing, and coupled with a brilliant vocabulary to inspire us to greatness in the kingdom of God. Shortly after he died, his wife gave me one of his Bibles, which I cherish.

I had concluded my freshman year of college when I first met the fourth man of great influence in my life. He approached me in the front of the auditorium where I had just performed in an epic biblical drama during a weekend of graduation exercises. He said, "Brother Stan, have you preached your first sermon yet?" I was immediately taken aback, first because nobody had ever called me "Brother Stan," and second, I certainly did not feel any calling to preach.

When I told him that I didn't know if I was called to preach, he assured me I need not worry about that. He proceeded to invite me to come to the church he served as pastor in Cincinnati, Ohio, to preach my inaugural message. Despite accepting his invitation, for many days afterward I was confused about that conversation. But he was so confident that this was what I should do that two months later, on August 5, 1976, I arrived at Calvary Church on Kemper Road in Cincinnati. During the preservice prayer meeting, many doubts circulated through my mind as I struggled with the whole idea of preaching and its implications for my future.

I was unprepared for how directly and clearly and personably God spoke to me in that prayer meeting. I was overwhelmed. I had walked into that prayer meeting with no sense of a call to preach on my life, but I walked out called and courageous. I am yet rejoicing over the man who was baptized at the conclusion of that message. I cannot tell you how many times I have wondered how differently my life would look today had not this astute pastor seen something in me that I couldn't see myself. I am indebted to him for picturing a preferred future for me. I have one of his Bibles, which I cherish.

The fifth formative influence in my life was my father-in-law. The first time I met him was the day I asked him for his daughter's hand in marriage. Had it not been for his older daughter paving the way for me and convincing him I was worth taking a chance on, it may not have gone so well. I knew he was a preacher, pastor, and former successful businessman with a powerful persona, but I had no idea how profoundly he would influence my life.

During our first year of marriage, my wife and I traveled throughout the Midwest while I served as an itinerant speaker. We would drive to my in-laws for a few days in between meetings. On such occasions, my father-in-law would invite me into his office, tell me stories about the ministry, and share sermons or scriptural thoughts he was working on. On one such occasion he told me there had been a time in his ministry—when his mind was younger and sharper—that if I quoted any verse in the Bible, he could tell me what book/chapter it was in.

In our fifth year of marriage, my wife and I were called to serve a small church in Wisconsin in a pastoral role. I asked my father-in-law to come and be the speaker at a meeting we were hosting for some area congregations. At the conclusion of his message, I was so impacted by his ministry and the evident spiritual authority he possessed that I knelt before him and asked him to pray a blessing over me. I cannot fully explain what happened in that moment, but I know for certain that something was transmitted to me that has stayed with me from that day forward. I have never been the same since. Little did we know that he would suddenly die of a heart attack just three months later. I have one of his Bibles, which I cherish.

I could say so much more about these five giants who imparted something unique and special into my life. I sincerely do not know where I would be today without their investment and impartation. I am not trying to impress anyone or claim that I am something special, but I would like to challenge you to look around and see who God has placed in your life. What young people are there right now who cannot see what you see in them? Are you going to make them pull themselves up by their own bootstraps, or will you invest your life in the next generation of leaders?

I'm so thankful that the men who mentored me were healthy, godly, balanced, and relational. They each conducted their lives on a high level. I believe that anointing flows downward. (See Ps. 133:1-3.) If you have any anointing from God in your life, you didn't get it all by yourself. The only way you can receive the anointing of God is to come under it. I was blessed to come under the anointing of these great men, and perhaps I carry with me, at least in part, a drop or two of their anointed lives.

As a church leader for the past forty-two years, I have come to appreciate the significance and blessing of observing emotionally and spiritually healthy people in leadership. Through the years I have served as a full-time evangelist, lead pastor, sectional youth director, district youth secretary, district global missions director, sectional presbyter, regional executive presbyter, district superintendent, and assistant general superintendent. As of this writing I have served on the general board of our organization for twenty-one years. I haven't seen it, all but I have certainly seen enough.

In a world of brokenness and human carnage, we need leaders who will check their baggage at the altar and not bring vestiges of dysfunction to the ministry, the pulpit, or to any phase of leadership in the church. Most of our conflicts are won or lost on the battlefield of our mind. Consequently, while in prayer, I routinely ask God to touch my mind, direct my thoughts, help me to think the right thoughts, read the right passages of scripture, read the right books, talk to the right people, and to surround myself with spiritual, healthy thinking so I can live a life and perform actions that please him.

I am on a mission to train the next generation of church leaders. I want the legacy of my early influencers to live on through me and flow downward to those I in turn invest my life in. Because of these mentors, I believe I also am living a life worth following. How about you?

CHAPTER 5

CHRISTLIKE LEADERS ARE ACCOUNTABLE

Then He appointed twelve, that they might be
with Him (Mark 3:14).

"Words show a man's wit, but action shows
his meaning."—Benjamin Franklin

Was Jesus accountable to anyone? Did his absolute power as God manifested in flesh corrupt absolutely? As God, Jesus didn't need accountability because he was never wrong, out of balance, inappropriate, deceived, indulgent, late, irresponsible, or any of the other human weaknesses that require accountability to overcome. But as man, Jesus was not above or beyond submitting himself to the Father, to his earthly parents, or even to his own followers.

Accountability is not just for the weak or vulnerable; it is good for everyone. We all perform better when someone we respect and have a relationship with is expecting us to do well. An accountability partner must be someone we hold in high regard—someone we do not want to disappoint. Our closest friend is probably not the best person for the role, because we need someone who will not give us a pass or look the other way when we fall short.

I have known talented, capable believers who did not want to be answerable to anyone. One young aspiring minister went to his pastor and said, "I've noticed lately that I can hardly stand to listen to anyone else preach. Do you reckon that means God is calling me to be a pastor?" I don't think that's a sure sign of a call to pastoral ministry, but some have launched out with even less.

I have watched licensed ministers seek out pastoral or church-leadership positions to show the world they have all the answers. Those who are moved to action in this way rarely, if ever, add value to anyone around them. Their performance never brings glory or growth to the kingdom of God. J. T. Pugh said, "If a man is bigger than the job, he will change the job, but if the job is bigger than he, the job will change him."

How many times have we seen this? People unqualified for positions of church leadership not only live in frustration, but they also frustrate the grace of God in most everything they do. Their elevated position confirms to them that they are exempt from accountability, which further empowers their unteachable spirit. Once church leaders become a law unto themselves, they never go anywhere but down.

Jesus was ready to lead early in life. At age twelve, he was already making an indelible impression on the theological brain trust of first-century Judea. When Mary and Joseph finally found him in the temple, they witnessed their son intelligently but respectfully discussing the scriptures with the doctors of the law. Had Jesus arrogantly displayed his superior knowledge and authority, these elders would not have granted him an audience.

Jesus's reply to his parents' subtle rebuke revealed his keen awareness of his mission and his accountability to it when he said, "I must be about my Father's business." What follows is astounding: "Then He went down with them and came to Nazareth, and was subject to them, but His mother kept all these things in her heart. And Jesus increased in wisdom and stature, and in favor with God and men" (Luke 2:51–52).

Jesus remained subject to his parents until he reached age thirty, the typical launch date of first-century rabbinical ministry. Yet freedom from the restraints of parental authority did not mean he cast off submission to others. He went straight to the Jordan River and submitted to the baptism of John, who had spent a lifetime of fasting, prayer, and sacrifice in the wilderness.

During his entire ministry, Jesus was careful to present himself as submitted and accountable. At a wedding celebration he deferred to his mother when she told him their hosts had run out of wine. He acknowledged that he did the bidding of his Father (John 12:49). He chose twelve to "be with him." (The rabbi/disciple relationship was based on mutual accountability.) His strong statements and subsequent interactions with Peter suggested accountability: (1) he asked Peter what he thought of him, (2) he gave Peter the keys to the kingdom, (3) he assured Peter that he had prayed for him, and (4) he asked Peter three times if he loved him. Even before Peter denied him, Jesus told this disciple that his faith would not fail, that he would be converted, that he would be profitable for the ministry, and that he would strengthen the brethren.

The fact that Jesus prayed demonstrated accountability. In his priestly prayer of John 17, Jesus showed deference to the Father. He demonstrated submission to authority when he prayed, "I have finished the work you sent me to do," and in Gethsemane, "If it is possible, let this cup pass from Me; nevertheless, not as I will, but as You will." Even while suffering on the cross, Jesus did not dismiss his strong sense of accountability to people who were close to him; he fulfilled the duty of an eldest son by placing his widowed mother in the care of John.

Jesus fulfilled his mission to the last detail. He remained submitted and accountable from birth to death. He never failed to do the right thing. For instance, after the resurrection, he returned to the very world that had crucified him and showed himself alive to his followers. Whether responding to critics, spending time with sinners, or associating with his disciples, he always reached for the right thing. In fact, it was said of him, "He has done all things well" (Mark 7:37).

Jesus Christ is the greatest accountability partner anyone could have. In fact, if someone has an intimate, meaningful, daily relationship with Jesus Christ, he or she will not need additional accountability. First, Jesus is the one who suffered, bled, died, rose again, saved us by his grace, and gave us everything we have. He is infinitely worthy of our respect. Second, how could we be disobedient on any night of the week, knowing we have a prayer tag-in with him the next morning?

Many books, podcasts, videos, and other media forms have expressed the need for accountability to overcome sin and weakness. Before accountability can work, however, the one desiring to be accountable must first of all respect and feel a keen sense of accountability to their partner (i.e., they do not want to let them down). Second, they must give their partner a list of a few questions that address their areas of weakness or temptation and give them verbal permission to ask those questions. The last question should always be, "Have you lied about anything you've just shared with me?" Third, there must be a regular, scheduled check-in time for the face-to-face accountability talk. When these principles are put in place and adhered to, it is amazing how powerful and effective accountability is.

However, I feel compelled to restate that the greatest accountability partner anyone could have been not your pastor, spouse, colleague, or best friend; it is Jesus Christ. He knows us better than anyone, yet he still loves us. He wants us to succeed, yet he is merciful if we fail. He never takes his eye off us and sees us when we win or lose. If someone feels a keen sense of accountability to Jesus and a conviction about not wanting to let him down, then accountability with Jesus works.

Many years ago, an acquaintance of mine told me that his wife had received a monetary gift for her birthday, so they decided to take a weekend trip. As they were driving past a casino she suddenly said, "I've never gambled in my life, but I'd like to go inside that casino just once to see what happens in there." Although this spontaneity was very unlike her, the husband pulled into the parking lot. When they entered the casino, to their amazement, they saw their former pastor and his wife at the blackjack table having a big night on the town—he in a tuxedo and she in a revealing evening gown. They were gambling for big money in a room hazy with smoke, free-flowing drinks, blaring club music, and hollow laughter.

On Sunday morning when this pastor arrives at his church office (after spending the previous night at an out-of-town casino), is he going to get down on his knees like every good pastor does and report in to Jesus? Is he going to tell how he's been a good steward of his time, how he's been spending God's gracious financial giving to him, how he and his wife are modeling godly behavior and temperance, and how he needs God's help to challenge the congregation that they should be denying ungodliness and worldly lusts and living soberly, righteously, and godly in the present age" (Titus 2:12)?

Then, when he stands before his congregation full of "Christ followers," what significant theological theme will he address? Separation, abstinence, moderation, conviction, holiness, modeling, modesty? Furthermore, what is next on his agenda? A trip to Bourbon Street for Mardi Gras? Pastors with lifestyles like this usually major on grace, not obedience.

Here is the point: how can a pastor of any stripe fool around on any night—much less Saturday night—knowing full well he is going to get up in the morning, walk to the platform, and deliver the precious word of the Lord to people who are trying to overcome their own indulgences, vices, and sinful pleasures? Spiritual leadership must be held to a higher standard: others can, but we cannot; others may, but we may not. Any church leader who lacks a keen sense of responsibility to live a life above reproach and a corresponding accountability to their Savior Jesus Christ is revealing that they have a religion and not a relationship.

Every pastor and church leader needs someone to answer to. Even those who feature themselves as apostles or prophets need accountability partners. Scripturally, it seems apparent that the first-century fivefold ministry practiced mutual accountability. Among the governmental ministry in the Acts of the Apostles account, there was no one apostle or prophet who had unique, untouchable status.

A clear example of this is in chapter 15, which describes a church leaders' council that convened in Jerusalem over the Gentile issue. Notably present were Paul (apostle to the Gentiles); Peter (apostle to the Jews); Barnabas (influential missionary, Antioch church leader, wealthy contributor, early mentor of Saul/Paul); and James, the local pastor, who was not one of the original twelve disciples. After a discussion of the resolutions on the table regarding the attempted Judaizing of Gentiles, it was James who prefaced his remarks with phrases like, "Wherefore I judge," "It seemed good to us and to the Holy Spirit," and "Listen to me..."

There was no power play at this council. No one attempted to gain the upper hand or play this issue for a political advantage. Everyone spoke what they felt the Lord was saying to them, but someone had to bring the matter to an equitable and peaceable conclusion. When James spoke, he was kind, diplomatic, wise, balanced, and pragmatic. He spoke from the position of consensus, both among his brethren, and their corporate resonance with the Holy Spirit.

We all live better lives with accountability in place. I am accountable to my Lord and Savior Jesus Christ. He gave me life, breath, and all things. I will answer to him at the judgment seat of Christ, but I also answer to him every day that I go to him in prayer and mutually examine my heart, spirit, and motives. He frequently lets me know whether or not I have done well. I am accountable to my wife of forty-three years. There is hardly an hour of any day that she does not know where I am or who I am with. I am accountable to our local church board for the overall operations of the congregation, including all finances, building projects, and business decisions.

When I was elected assistant general superintendent in our ministerial organization, I sought a conversation with the general superintendent and submitted myself to his spiritual oversight and authority in my life. We were in Panama at a meeting with our top leaders from around the world. Following a powerful message and communion, while others were praying with each other, he laid his hands on my head and prayed over me. That was eleven years ago, but to this day I yet sense that covering in my life. Additionally, ever since I was in my late twenties, my older brother (a long-tenured pastor) has been my pastoral covering and who possesses veto power over me. I stay in touch with these men who bring expertise and wisdom to the table and who pray for me.

Having served as an elected official in our organization for thirty years, I have been in the position to observe a few men who did and said the "right things" to get elected to pastoral positions. Once they gained the trust of church members, however, they switched to their hidden agenda, dismissed the church board (made up of faithful men in the congregation), and replaced them with like-minded cronies from around the country (there is usually no accountability in this arrangement). When all checks and balances were gone, they felt empowered to rule like kings over their powerless subjects. Scenarios like this predictably end in disaster.

My question is, what about the well-meaning saints of God who are unknowingly subjected to such autocratic rulers? These people have raised their families in the church, built the building, paid the bills—and long after the tsunami of tyrannical leadership subsides, they are left to clean up the mess. Do they have any recourse or appeal? Do they know the terms of the church bylaws or whether they have any options other than leaving? Do they feel betrayed and become embittered against all spiritual leadership? Do they forsake their walk with God? If they try to ask honest questions about the changes being made, are they met with statements like "Touch not the Lord's anointed and do his prophets no harm," or they are ostracized and dismissed?

When I served as district superintendent, it fell my lot to confront such a situation. I called a pastor with a less-than-two-year tenure to ask questions about the rumors I'd been hearing. He confirmed that he was taking his congregation in "another direction"; he wanted more control and less interference from the organization. This told me he wanted to answer to no one for what he was planning to do.

I informed him that the congregation had done just fine for fifty-four years under previous administrations without interference or power grabs from the organization. He then let me know that his new direction was more pleasing to God than the old, implying that the previous administrations and the affiliated organization were not meeting his threshold of holiness. The sincere church members did not know what else to do but follow along and voted to remove their affiliation.

I was very troubled but powerless to intervene. It gave me no satisfaction to inform the local presbyter that I felt certain this man was hiding something. It took two years and a few spiritual casualties until one night he skipped town after it was revealed he had molested a female minor. One of his adjunct board members was busted in a sex sting operation. If you are living a godly life and someone or something around you doesn't feel right, it probably isn't.

I conclude this chapter with a leadership allegory borrowed from Dr. Seuss, who wrote *Yertle the Turtle*, one of my favorite children's books. All the turtles in the pond were content to live and let live. However, Yertle's ambition, coupled with his insecurities and insatiable hunger for power, inspired him to demand that every other turtle in the pond subordinate to his authority. No one dared question his demands. They all obeyed as he yelled at them to lift him up by forming a stack of turtles beneath him. As he ascended higher with each additional turtle in the stack, he boasted that he was king of all he could see.

One turtle begged Yertle to reconsider and release them from this tyranny, but instead he placed more demands upon them. All of the turtles in the pond became miserable. They realized they had been duped into supporting a one-turtle show. They found no satisfaction in the life he was requiring of them. The little pond they had enjoyed up until now had been taken from them without any recourse.

The story then zeroes in on a humble, polite turtle (named "Mack") who, at the bottom of the stack, was struggling under a load he was not able to bear. Without warning, he suddenly burped. This involuntary disruption unbalanced the entire stack and they all came tumbling down, with Yertle having the farthest to fall. And that was the end of King Yertle's ridiculous reign. So take a lesson from Dr. Seuss: if you are not following the leadership model of Jesus Christ, and everyone under you us miserable, all it usually takes is something as slight as a hiccup for your house of cards to come tumbling down. May it never be so with us.

CHAPTER 6

CHRISTLIKE LEADERS
PRACTICE SELF-CARE

*The report went around concerning Him all
the more; and great multitudes came together to
hear, and to be healed by Him of their infirmities.
So He Himself often withdrew into the wilderness
and prayed (Luke 5:15–16).*

"A man who wants to lead an orchestra
must turn his back on the crowd."—Unknown

Jesus's life on earth was remarkable in every way. His ministry lasted
only forty-two months, during which he was constantly under
pressure to meet demands from religious leaders, family members,
and the needy public. On more than one occasion he was asked to
leave the area after teaching, preaching, and performing miracles of
healing and deliverance from demonic oppression.

The contrast in the above text is striking: great multitudes
came to hear and be healed...yet he withdrew into the wilderness
and prayed. We don't know if Jesus was an introvert or an extrovert;
however, we do know he didn't rely on crowds or caffeine for his
energy source. It's a rare introverted leader who could attract such a

crowd, and a rare extroverted leader who could walk away from such a crowd. Suffice it to say that Jesus was not seduced by applause nor was he discouraged by disapproval.

It is remarkable how the people of Gadara responded to Jesus after he delivered the demoniac man and restored him to tranquility. One moment the crazed man was terrorizing the community, roving naked among the tombs, breaking chains and rattling shackles; the next moment Jesus was casting a legion of devils out of him. The devils asked to enter a large herd of swine. The herd ran wildly over a precipice and plunged into the sea where they drowned.

In the next scene, this man is radically changed: he's clothed, in his right mind, and sitting at the feet of Jesus. One would have thought the entire population would have come out to celebrate this dramatic occurrence, that they would have hosted a deliverance party and welcomed this man back to his family and friends, that Jesus would have been given great honor. But their unexpected reaction serves as a stark reminder to all that not everyone in our community appreciates the work we do. Incredulously, the Gadarenes asked Jesus to leave the area. They were more concerned about the pork market and their pocketbooks than they were about the broken people of their community having their sanity and peace restored.

A pastor once told the story about a church in upstate New York that was impacting a group of young, new believers. These kids were coming off the streets and were being delivered from sin and every vice imaginable. The church's worship facility had no air-conditioning, so during the heat of that summer they would open the doors and windows during services. The neighbors began to complain about the loud music and boisterous worship. On more than one occasion the police came and kindly asked them to quiet down.

The pastor finally had enough of the complaints, so he took one of the recently converted young men with him down to the police station and asked to see the captain. As they sat in the captain's office the pastor rehearsed the menace that this young man had previously been to the community: drugs, DUIs, burglaries, vandalism, court appearances, and jail time. His irresponsible behavior had cost the taxpayers untold grief and thousands of dollars in court costs and jail time. Yet the police captain could easily see the humility and respect portrayed by the young man sitting his office.

Finally, the pastor said, "Look, Captain. This kid is no longer terrorizing our community, and if every kid in our neighborhood was like this kid, no one would have to lock their doors at night. You couldn't fix him, you couldn't change him, and you couldn't do anything for him despite all your arrests and programs. What you couldn't seem to get done in years of failed attempts, Jesus did in one night, and it didn't cost you or the taxpayers one dime." The captain was impressed, and he became an ally and defender of the church as they kept on making a difference through the power of Christ.

An important part of self-care in leadership is not to allow a lack of appreciation or recognition disturb your peace and make you feel unappreciated. When Jesus saw the reaction of the Gadarenes, he simply got back in the boat and sailed away. Don't wait around for photo ops every time you go the extra mile to make a difference in someone's life. Your job is not to anticipate rewards for good deeds but to always do the right thing, no matter who is watching or who takes time to say thanks.

I'll go one step further. After performing a notable miracle, Jesus occasionally would request, if not command, the overjoyed recipients to tell no one what he had done for them. It would have been virtually impossible for a former demoniac or cleansed leper to explain how they had regained their physical or spiritual health without speaking of their encounter with Jesus. Jesus's reason for his attempted censuring of their testimonies was to curb the enthusiasm of casual gawkers, sensation seekers, and fickle multitudes. Jesus understood that his heightened popularity would agitate his detractors and rush their judgment of him before it was time.

Jesus, as God manifested in flesh, had unlimited resources. However, because he was also human in every way, he needed to manage his resources much like we do. He required rest, food, personal space, and time to reenergize. Constantly aware of his energy level, he would either wade into needy people or retreat, depending on the expediency of the moment. In fact, one day he was in a crowd of needy people and suddenly felt virtue flow out of him. He instantly knew that someone had touched him with purpose.

You might say that Jesus guarded his energy. Author Laurie Beth Jones suggested that Jesus was so "clear about His mission that He avoided many real and potential energy leaks."[7] She reasoned that "even though he was a teacher, He refused to engage in meaningless debates with critics who wanted only to argue and not learn." Even at his trial, he did not waste time, energy, or words in what he knew would be a useless defense. Even though he was a recruiter of sorts, he never wasted energy begging or manipulating others to follow him. In fact, he trained his disciples to "wipe the dust from their feet" and keep moving if people were resistant to his mission.

He instructed his team to not "'cast your pearls before swine,' a very graphic image about the importance of knowing where and with whom to share the treasure of your energy." Jones then gave a warning to leaders: "How many energy leaks do we have in our own daily lives? Leaks such as angry words, distractions, or tampering in someone else's business while neglecting our own…leaders must therefore be aware that their energy is subject to depletion, and they must make guarding that energy reserve a priority."[8]

An anonymous person once said, "The first rule of winning is don't beat yourself." I have colleagues who can miss a night of sleep and keep going all the next day. I've had friends who would be arriving at the prime time of their day just as I was crawling into bed. This is not good; the old timers used to say that nothing good happens after midnight. By the grace of God, I have always been able to sleep. Even during some of my darkest seasons, God has given me rest.

Church leaders should be sensitive to their energy and endurance level. On numerous occasions during seasons of intense circumstances, I have heard or felt an inner signal telling me it was time for a break. It's like an internal barometer that lets me know I'm at my limit. Every time I sense the signal, I check out for a time of renewal.

---

[7] Laurie Beth Jones, *Jesus CEO* (New York, NY: Hyperion, 1995), 21–22.

[8] Ibid., 23.

That break could be something as simple as a nap in my office chair, retreating to some pleasure reading, a trip to the golf course, going to lunch with my wife or a friend, or taking an unscheduled day off. Perhaps this is at least one reason why my marriage, my home, and my ministry enjoy a climate of peace. Of course, weather occurs and storms rage, but the overarching climate is peace.

Immediately after returning from his baptism and subsequent forty-day fast in the wilderness, which culminated in an encounter with the devil, Jesus entered the synagogue in his hometown of Nazareth. It must have been a proud moment for Mary when her son was invited to read from the scriptures. The selected passage was taken from Isaiah's prophecy concerning Messiah (Luke 4:17–20). After reading it, Jesus informed his audience that he had come to fulfill this prophecy by bringing the gospel, healing the broken, delivering captives, recovering sight for the blind, liberating the bruised, and preaching the Year of Jubilee.

The crowd became outraged. "You're no messiah, you're Joseph's son!" They force-marched him to the brow of a precipice, intending to push him over the edge to his death. In this moment in his early ministry, Jesus understood the need to establish boundaries with those around him. The scripture says, "Then passing through the midst of them, He went His way" (Luke 4:30). Considering the agitation of his audience and the fact that they were pushing him toward the edge, we can well assume that Jesus had to temporarily (and supernaturally) immobilize the angry mob, thus enabling himself to pass through them without incident.

Even the humble, meek, obedient, submitted, suffering servant, Jesus Christ, would not allow the people he came to save to control his agenda. He planned his calendar, ran his life, fulfilled every prophecy, met every deadline, and—despite his short tenure—finished his work (John 17:4).

Too many excellent ministers have failed to practice good self-care; they have allowed dysfunctional people to maneuver them to the point of giving up or muscle them to the precipice to be pushed into an early demise. More than one God-called man or woman has been badgered to the brink of brokenness. Crazy people can drive well people to the point they feel they themselves are the problem.

I was raised in a Christian home. My parents were authentic, and my older siblings loved and supported me and each other. We had boundaries, we enjoyed fellowship, there was no abusive behavior, we were kind and respectful to each other, and love and acceptance was all around us. I think I can speak for my siblings when I say that our heroes were not public figures or pop-culture icons; our heroes were all in the church. When you are raised in a loving, healthy, and balanced family culture, it's a rude awakening to discover that there are mean, ill-mannered, disrespectful bullies sitting in church pews.

When I was a young pastor, elected at age twenty-five, I thought that if I would just pray and fast more, be a good Christ follower, love everyone, and study the word of God that everyone would love and follow me. It was a rude awakening to realize that no good deed goes unpunished when toxic people are around. Everything I did or said added fuel to the fire: my manner of speech was criticized, my ministerial calling was questioned, my doctrinal integrity was doubted, and my leadership was thwarted on every side.

This congregation had not baptized anyone in two years prior to the arrival of my family. But by the grace of God, we baptized sixteen new people in our first three months. I assumed the church people would be glad because they had elected us to lead them into revival and growth. Instead, the church board called a meeting to terminate my tenure. Had it not been for a prayer meeting going on in the sanctuary, the good will and words of my presbyter, and divine intervention, that meeting may have been the end of my assignment there.

On three occasions I sought forgiveness from a board member (once going to his house), each time without fully understanding what I had done to inspire his vehement opposition. My uninformed but intentional efforts to make peace were met with more accusations, complaints, and hostilities. I later understood that his rancor was inspired by my lack of promoting him in the congregation, once again demonstrating that the perceived problem is usually not the problem.

One night after our midweek service, I inadvertently discovered that this elder had undergone quintuple bypass surgery earlier that day. Although it seemed obvious his family had not wanted the pastor to know, I stopped by the hospital to see him on my way home from church. Somebody must have given the family a tip-off because one of his sons met me in the front lobby and snidely asked, "Why are you here?" When I said, "I've come to pray for your father," he said flatly, "We won't allow you to do that." I politely left him and walked toward the emergency entrance. His daughter met me there and after scolding me, she said, "You're the reason my father had to have heart surgery!"

In forty-three years of full-time ministry, that was the only time I "shook the dust off my feet." I shared this with an older pastor and district leader during a private lunch. Knowing the people I was dealing with, he chuckled and said, "Well, Stan, up to now you've let these people run over you and wipe their feet on you like a doormat, but you'll probably never let it happen again."

One of the occupational hazards of pastoral ministry is that we want everyone to be successful Christians. We appreciate the pastoral care and mentoring we received from others. Our natural assumption is that if it worked for us, it will work for them. The hard reality, however, is that it won't work in every case, despite our best efforts. Jesus spoke a powerful truth about the human condition when he said, "You have the poor with you always" (Matt. 26:11). Some people are more satisfied with old problems than they are with new solutions, and they will be happy to take up your time to explain why. One elderly retired pastor was asked what he would change, if anything, in all the years of his ministry. He replied saucily, "I wouldn't spend as much time with the nuts."

Author Gary Thomas warned that those in the ministry need to learn how to "play defense." He admitted that for most of his ministry he only "played offense." One day a friend encouraged him to study Jesus and notice that "He walked away from people many times."[9] Thomas went on to observe that Paul, Peter, and John (the apostle of love), warned others to "beware of certain toxic individuals." He observed that the four Gospel writers recorded that on no less than two dozen occasions Jesus walked away; or if others walked away, he didn't chase after them.

Thomas wrote, "There are certain people who drain us, demean us, and distract us from other healthy relationships. Long after they're gone, we're still fighting with them in our minds and trying to get them out of our hearts. They keep us awake. They steal our joy. They demolish our peace. They make us weaker spiritually. They even invade our times of worship and pervert them into season of fretting." He clinched his argument for walking away from toxic people by saying, "What if there's another way at looking at how we handle toxic people in our lives? What if the way and work of Christ are so compelling, so urgent, and so important that allowing ourselves to become bogged down by toxic people is an offense to God rather than a service to God?"

One day while praying and talking to God, I had an epiphany of sorts about challenges I was facing from toxic people. I was searching my heart and checking my spirit to see if there was any behavior or attitude in me that was creating the toxicity. The Lord seemed to say to me, "Are you submitted to me? Do you stay in my word? Are you being led by my Spirit? Are you under spiritual authority? Do you possess a humble, repentant spirit? Do you imitate the attitude that was in me?" After I checked all these boxes and responded with a humble yes, I then heard, "You are not the 'crazy' one. Their problem is not with you; it is with me. They are doing none of the things you are doing and do not have the attitude toward me that you have." As a result, I am learning when to walk away.

We must become better at self-care. For instance, I'm concerned that we have not observed the spirit of the sabbath. Sabbaths and sabbaticals were designed by God to increase our fruitfulness and deepen our faith along the way. The sabbath is a declaration that God has finished his creative work. No one needs to add to it, and

---

9   Gary Thomas, *When to Walk Away* (Grand Rapids, MI: Zondervan, 2019), 11.

no one should try, because no one can. God's people were instructed to follow his example by doing nothing to advance their own cause on the scheduled day of rest. It was the only aspect of God's creative ability that his creatures could imitate. They could not create, but they could rest.

Since the sabbath acknowledges the completed work of God, working on the sabbath may be communicating that what we are doing on the sabbath is as important as what God did at creation. Refraining from working on the sabbath simply expresses that our work is insignificant compared to his. Our ministry activities and other benevolent activities should always give way to his design for the sabbath day.

The fact of the matter is that the work will never be done. There will always be more to do. When Jesus cried out, "It is finished" at the young age of thirty-three, he was sending a message to us that there will never be enough time to do what we want to do, but there will always be enough time to do the will of God. So the Sabbath rest is a command we respond to and not a result of there being nothing left to do. It is a part of our obedience, not a consequence of our expedience and industriousness. The work will never be done.

The primary purpose of the sabbath was to rest. After six days of creation, God rested on the seventh day. He instituted the seventh day as a day of rest, renewal, and recovery. He also instituted the sabbatical year and stated that in that year, the land was to lie fallow in order to rest and be replenished. He promised the Israelites they would reap a bumper crop in the sixth year, enough to sustain them through the seventh year and into the planting season of the new cycle. God also instituted the Year of Jubilee, which was a celebration of seven sabbatical years. All prisoners were to be released, all debts forgiven, and all land restored to its original family.

The sabbatical institution was God's way of giving Israel a reset. The sabbath idea was a revelation of how God expected kingdom business to be conducted. For example, he understood what hope-lessness would do to the human condition. The Year of Jubilee would remove despair and foster hope for recovery in the future. It should be noted, however, that there is no record in the scriptures or in

69

rabbinical history that Israel ever celebrated the sabbatical year or the Year of Jubilee. Perhaps their attitude was that observing the sabbatical and jubilee years would cost too much. It appears they were unwilling to forgive their debtors, surrender procured property, forgo a year of harvest, or release their prisoners (servants).

Could it be that their failure to observe the sabbatical year for four hundred and ninety years is what sent them into Babylonian captivity for seventy years? God exacted from the Israelites what they had refused to give to him willingly. The land finally had the rest that God prescribed, but Israel did not benefit from it. I wonder what price we are paying for not practicing God's law of rest and recovery. The price for failing to practice self-care is great—to us personally, to our marriage, to our children, and to our congregation. How many ministerial marriages could have been saved, how many PKs (preachers' kids) and MKs (missionary's kids) could have avoided brokenness, how many tenures could have been extended, how many cases of infidelity would have never happened had we been honoring the spirit of the sabbath?

Some religious cultures are not good at resting. When I was a young minister, I heard our top leader state that he had never taken a vacation. The second top leader's wife said their summer vacations were spent at the many camp meetings where her husband was the speaker. That's a vacation? Eating every meal with your hosts, attending church twice a day, staying on the grounds in somebody's used RV or cinderblock dorm room, walking a good distance in your bathrobe (in front of God and everybody) to take a shower? Apparently, that sounds spiritual to some people but not to me.

The best advice I have found for church leaders on practicing sabbath rest is to divert daily (even for an hour); withdraw weekly (take a day off); quarantine quarterly (get out of town for a night or two); abandon annually (family vacation); and if at all possible, go on a literal sabbatical every few years (which I have never done). A sabbatical is not a vacation; it is an intentionally determined amount of time set aside to accomplish a ministerial goal beyond the norm.

A recent report estimated that there is as much stress on a typical individual in a twenty-four-hour period today as there was in an entire year a generation ago. Some of our technological conveniences are contributors to stress. One source of daily stress is self-inflicted and held in the palm of your hand: your smartphone. Smartphones can become detrimental to self-care. You hold the world in your hands. Just look around in any public place and see people's eyes glued to the face of their phone. We are bombarded by social-media notifications and unsolicited marketing texts and e-mails. I would say that most smartphone users have unknowingly become addicted to them, absentmindedly reaching for them in every unoccupied moment.

I have been sitting with friends during lunch and suddenly see them bolt from the table, mumbling something about inadvertently having left their cell phone in their car. The first time this happened, I thought to myself, *How silly. You mean you can't go an hour without your phone at your side?* But now I confess… I have since done the same.

The average pastor today is much more accessible and therefore vulnerable than he/she was a generation ago. Sundays alone are challenging enough, especially with multiple services. The Commodores sang the hit song "Easy Like Sunday Morning." Obviously, Lionel Richie was never a pastor. Doc Mckenzie wrote the song "I'll Be Alright," which included the oft-repeated line, "Every day will be like Sunday." I can assure you this song never comforted a church leader. We want to go to a heaven where every day will be like Monday, not Sunday.

Occasionally I have been overwhelmed with the sense that everyone wanted a piece of me—and that was before I owned a smartphone. On the one hand, texting is wonderful because you control the response time, and it can be much quicker than a phone call; on the other hand, anybody who has your number can at any time decide to invade your space, divert your attention, or perhaps ruin your day. I have 2,500 cell phone numbers in my database. It is not unusual for me to engage 2,000 text messages in one billing cycle. Yet I consider myself fortunate because the average for millennials is 3,800. If all the social messaging platforms are included, there are 145 billion messages sent every day worldwide.[10]

Having a cell phone means it is virtually impossible for a church leader to not bring their work home with them. Years ago, *Leadership Magazine* featured a cartoon of a pastor coming home at the end of the day, being trailed by many members of the congregation. His wife met him at the door with the exasperated comment, "How many times have I told you not to bring your work home with you!"

Before cell phones I thought caller ID was the greatest thing since sliced bread. I could see who was calling and decide whether I wanted to answer. We still have that feature on our cell phones; however, the calls and text messages now come through while we're using our phone for personal reading, taking notes, perusing social media, or entertainment. Even though we may not respond immediately, our privacy has been invaded and our professional courtesy to respond is now lurking in the back of our mind.

Is there such a thing as cell phone addiction? Yes, I believe there is. Research demonstrates that excessive cell phone use can lead to low self-esteem, low impulse control, anxiety, and depression. I wonder how many of these symptoms are induced not only by the sheer saturation of technology and accessibility people are exposed to, but also by their poor choices of entertainment. Most of the cases I'm aware of regarding inappropriate sexual behavior involve the use of a cell phone (porn, sexting, lewd text threads, spouse discovering their mate has been cheating, etc.).

Would you like to be free of clinical depression? Would you like to avoid burnout? Would you like to bypass a nervous breakdown? Would you like to escape moral failure? Would you like to rejuvenate your physical body? Would you like to charge up your spiritual batteries?

A doctor of behavioral psychology told me that 90 percent of all patients in mental treatment centers are there because of a deep-rooted forgiveness issue. He also said that going without sleep for forty-eight hours can cause a person to become clinically insane.

---

[10] textrequest.com.

Being willing to forgive and taking time to rest are just two of the many disciplines we can control that will improve our mental, physical, and spiritual health—but we dismiss them all too easily.

Many in church leadership see their job/calling as detrimental to their overall mental and spiritual health as well as to that of their family. One small group of pastors was asked the question: "What do you fear the most?" As they each answered in turn, tears began to flow freely, and several couldn't even finish their answer. One admitted he didn't know how much longer his marriage could sustain the pressure. But another leader's answer was particularly troubling. He said, "I just don't want my kids growing up hating God because of me."

In their significant work *Pastors at Greater Risk*,[11] H. B. London Jr. and Neil B. Wiseman offer some startling statistics regarding ministers:

1. Eighty percent believe pastoral ministry affects their families negatively.
2. Thirty-three percent say that being in ministry is an outright hazard to their family.
3. Seventy-five percent report they've had a significant stress-related crisis at least once in their ministry.
4. Fifty percent feel unable to meet the needs of the job.
5. Ninety percent feel they're inadequately trained to cope with ministry demands.
6. Twenty-five percent of pastors' wives see their husband's work schedule as a source of conflict. Those in ministry are equally likely to have their marriage end in divorce as general church members. The clergy has the second highest divorce rate among all professions.
7. Eighty percent of pastors say they have insufficient time with their spouse.
8. Fifty-six percent of pastors' wives say they have no close friends.

---

[11] H. B. London Jr. and Neil B. Wiseman (Ventura, CA: Regal Books, 2003).

9. Forty-five percent of pastors' wives say the greatest danger to them and their family is physical, emotional, mental, and spiritual burnout.
10. Fifty-two percent of pastors say they and their spouses believe that being in pastoral ministry is hazardous to their family's well-being and health.
11. Forty-five percent of pastors say they've experienced depression or burnout to the extent they needed to take a leave of absence from ministry.
12. Seventy percent of pastors say they do not have someone they consider a close friend.

Many years ago, a former colleague tragically fell prey to adultery. In his autobiography, R. J. Bell said something that should shake every church leader to the core: "I could not answer in a fifteen-word sentence why I committed adultery, but I would have to say that a series of things came together in my life that made adultery possible."[12]

Bell cited a study by Francis A. Schaeffer Institute of Church Leadership (FASICLD):

> Eighty-nine percent of the pastors we surveyed considered leaving the ministry. Fifty-seven percent said they would leave if they had a better place to go, including secular work. One hundred percent said they had a close associate or seminary buddy who had left the ministry because of burnout, conflict in their church, or moral failure. Thirty-five percent leave the ministry, most after only five years.

Accountability does not guarantee perfection, but it certainly is one significant piece in the profile of integrity. One study conducted

---

[12] R. J. Bell, *Your Pastor Needs This Book: 5 huge mistakes you can help your pastor avoid* (Four Bells Publishing, 2012).

by a Christian research group revealed the profile of moral failure in the ministry. They solicited anonymous responses from ministry leaders who invited the ravages of adultery into their marriage. Once the results were tallied, they filtered all the dynamics of hundreds of failures down to three telling characteristics: the feeling of isolation, accountability to no one, a nonexistent prayer life.

In my own personal knowledge and experience with colleagues and friends in the ministry who have strayed down the path of immorality, I can say these results resonate with my observations. At a conference attended by thousands of ministers and spouses, I addressed the profile of moral failure in the ministry. While I was preaching, the daughter of a fallen pastor leaned over to her husband and said, "That's exactly what happened to Dad."

One minister that I grew up with became a pastor and then was elected district youth president. The week I was speaking at the youth camp under his supervision, he was rendezvousing with his partner in adultery (his choir director). A few weeks later his sin found him out. I intentionally connected with him a few months later and asked him how it happened. My question was not only to demonstrate an interest in his story and recovery, but also for my desire to examine my own life. He said, "Our church was growing, I was being celebrated in my city and my district, and we were launching a building program. I suppose that I became intoxicated on success, I got busy, and I guess I just...stopped...praying."

This chapter may not contain everything you need to know to practice good self-care, but I hope it will inspire you to look deep inside, be honest with yourself, and make lifestyle decisions today that could save your marriage, your family, your ministry, and your soul. If nothing else, may this chapter serve as an alarm if you see some of the warning signs of ministerial or moral danger. Take care of yourself; nobody else can.

CHAPTER 7

CHRISTLIKE LEADERS PURSUE PEACE

> *On that very day some Pharisees came, saying to Him, "Get out and depart from here, for Herod wants to kill You." And He said to them, "Go, tell that fox, 'Behold, I cast out demons and perform cures today and tomorrow, and the third day I shall be perfected.' Nevertheless I must journey today, tomorrow, and the day following; for it cannot be that a prophet should perish outside of Jerusalem (Luke 13:31–33).*

"A man who rules his spirit is greater than a man who takes a city."—Solomon

Jesus conducted his public and personal life under a banner of peace. Of course, he was and is the Prince of Peace, not in title only but also in authority and practice. He refused to let the devil, the Pharisees, Herod, Pilate, or any other detractor hold sway over his emotions or responses to their attacks. He was always in control of himself, he always ruled his own spirit, and he always chose his attitude. When Judas betrayed him, Jesus merely asked, "Judas, are you betraying the Son of Man with a kiss?" When five thousand men plus women and children walked away during and after his sermon, his only reaction was to turn to his disciples and ask, "Do you plan to leave too?" When Peter went back to fishing in Galilee after the resurrection, Jesus made a point to be there, take him aside, asking gently, "Peter, do you love me?"

It is the will of God that his kingdom operates in peace. Peace becomes the culture of those living in obedience and submission to God, his word, and his will. Of course, life presents challenges to our peace. Living in peace does not mean the absence of conflict any more than a stormy day in a mild climate zone. Those who live on the Gulf Shore understand that hurricanes happen, but not every day. I live in "tornado alley" where we have had many close calls, but not every day. Weather ultimately succumbs to climate as should conflict to the climate of God-given peace.

Perhaps the most underrated weapon of spiritual warfare available to us is peace. We typically don't think of peace as a weapon, but I can assure you that it is. Peace sounds weak and anemic to a certain class of leaders. I have been acquainted with some church leaders who are quite comfortable in chaos. If all hell is not breaking loose somewhere in their lives, they will find a way to break it loose.

Some leaders have learned to lead without peace, despite God's best efforts, their family's best efforts, and even their congregation's best efforts to the contrary. Chaos seems to gravitate to them in their personal life, in their congregation, and among their circle of friends. This type of leadership is either constantly in a battle, coming out of a battle, or going back in to another battle. Their leadership style just seems to draw fire.

Some speakers go to the pulpit looking for a fight. Their tendency to preach and teach against things they don't like or aren't good at, even though they have no context in scripture, has always amazed me. For example, when I first married Marlene, she was quick to inform me that her dad preached against the game of golf and advised me not to tell him that I played. But I decided I was not going to sneak around, hiding my golf clubs from his view. I couldn't be worried about opening my trunk in his presence with my clubs in view or hiding them in my garage when her parents came to visit.

I went straight to Marlene's dad and told him that I meant no disrespect by occasionally enjoying a round of golf with friends. I asked him if he had ever played, and he said no. I explained that golf no longer held the stigma that it had when he was young. It was no longer just a rich man's game; I could walk eighteen holes for four dollars and twenty-five cents. I could play without gambling, and I could go into the clubhouse without sitting at the bar. Golf was a fellowship game to be enjoyed on a beautifully situated, well-groomed golf course created by God and man. He hitched up his belt with both hands, stroked his chin, then sheepishly said, "Well, I suppose you playing golf is no worse than me drinking an entire pot of coffee at one sitting, is it?" I assume he was conceding that we all have our "vices," which I thought was an honest concession on his part. We never discussed it again.

I learned a long time ago that what you are against may get a response and attract some followers, but being contrary is not a sustainable vision. I once watched an I'm-against-it brand of leadership create division and leave a large church organization because it was not spiritual enough for their taste. They founded their own organization on the aspects they didn't like about their mother organization. During the twenty years of its existence, the members began devouring one another, became fragmented, then completely disintegrated. Proverbs 29:18 (KJV) says, "Where there is no vision, the people perish." I would add that without a compelling and positive vision, the people will go to another parish. Furthermore, perish the thought if your vision is only what you are against!

I once knew a pastor who had a unique way of motivating his congregation: reveal the enemy, rally the troops, and raise an offering. He typically would first expose a doctrine or practice espoused by some other leader or organization. His critique could range from the enemy's view of the eschaton to whether or not there were modern-day apostles or perhaps to their preferred brand of Christian music. He then would identify proponents of such alleged apostasies and create arguments against them and their delusion. Finally, he would use such an occasion to raise an offering to support some project he wanted to get done. Sadly, it seemed to work.

I watched years later that same elder soften his criticism of the style of Christian music he had previously attacked, all because it better suited his needs at that time. Someone called this "The Grandfather Clause," meaning you no longer preach against the things your grandchildren are now doing. If there is anything that can discourage good people, it is to see inconsistencies exposed in leadership because of convenience or familial relationships.

A church leader can create an issue-oriented culture if he/she is always finding fault with people, other churches, and organizations. Issue-oriented communicators typically do not need to study and prepare their presentations; all they need to incite an anxious response from their audience is something or someone to be against, even if all they can come up with is the devil. It's always easy to get an "amen" or solicit a response when preaching against Satan.

Leadership built on the constant raising of issues is unsustainable. A steady diet of negative preaching, finger-pointing, or calling-out of things you don't like may solicit cheap "amens," but it also will attract a certain mentality of people that will never impact a community. I heard the story years ago about a backward country preacher who, in conversation, was badmouthing the big city church. He said, "Yeah, that big church uptown has a high steeple, big fancy doors, stained glass windows, insurance salesmen, airplane pilots, and professionals. And all we get around here is a bunch of dingbats...and those dingbats bring more dingbats." I suppose he proved once again that you can't attract what you want, but you will attract what you are.

A church leader's home should be marked with peace. I first learned about the power of peace in my childhood home. My parents led us four children in the discipline of peace. My father valued peace and placed a high premium upon it. One day I was telling some of my cousins about how my dad would typically break up a fight between us siblings by singing a made-up song. The lyrics were repeated four times to a simple melody: "We love each other, yes we do."

When I started singing the song in fun, one of my cousins gasped and exclaimed, "You know that song? I thought my mother [my dad's sister] made it up." At that moment, we compared notes and figured out that our grandmother apparently had composed that song while attempting to restore peace to her children (our parents) that were fighting. I received a revelation: I am the benefactor of generational peacemakers. And now, so are my children.

I have tried to navigate my life on the pathway of peace. My wife and I have tried to raise our children under a banner of peace. We value peace, we work toward peace, we protect peace, and we operate in peace. In the early 1990s, we built a home and lived there for eight years. During that time God blessed us with two more children, so we sold and purchased a larger house to accommodate four children. A few days after we vacated our old house, the lady who bought it called my wife and asked, "Who *are* you people?"

My wife answered, "What do you mean?"

The lady said, "Well, I don't know who you are, but you have left something behind in this house I have never felt before."

My wife said, "What do you think it is?"

The lady said, "I feel peace in this house!"

Why is it that 90 percent of all arguments in Christian homes occur either while getting ready for church, on the way to church, or in the church parking lot? A third-grade Sunday school teacher asked her class where God lived.

One little girl blurted out, "God lives in our bathroom."

This was too good to pass up, so with a smile the teacher asked, "How do you know that?"

The little girl answered, "Well, every Sunday morning when we're getting ready for church, my dad pounds on the bathroom door and shouts, 'My god, are you still in there?'"

Peace is a culture that must continually be initiated and reinforced. When peace reigns in a home, the rewards are priceless. When chaos conquers and the family is going in all directions at once, the consequences are costly. I love peace. I covet peace. I cherish peace. Paul said, "Follow after the things which make for peace" (Rom. 14:19, KJV). Therefore, I follow after peaceful things: peaceful music, peaceful literature, peaceful entertainment choices, peaceful leisurely activities, peaceful people to spend time with, and so forth.

A family was on the way home from church one Sunday when one of the boys in the back seat began to cry. The dad asked, "Son, what's wrong with you?"

The boy wiped his eyes and said, "Well, Dad, you heard the pastor this morning. He said every child in our church deserves to go home with a family where there is love, joy, and peace…but I want to stay with you guys."

A friend once told me that for thirty years he had never once looked forward to going home. I still cannot comprehend that. He felt safer outside his home than inside. My home has always been the opposite. There have been days that I've raced home in my car, lowered the garage door, run into the house, quickly closed the door behind me, and leaned against it with a deep sigh. I felt like I had entered a sanctuary. I owe the sanctuary spirit of our home to God's grace and my dear wife.

In fact, not too long ago, on a day when I wasn't at home, two men knocked on our door to deliver a refrigerator. Marlene said that one of them was sort of strutting through the living room when suddenly he stopped dead in his tracks, saying, "Whoa, something's in this house."

My wife said, "What do you mean?"

He looked around nervously and said, "I feel something in this house."

She said, "Oh, I know what that is. You're feeling the presence of Jesus Christ."

He said, "Ma'am, that is exactly what it is."

I have thought about that many times. I can't say that it feels like the holy of holies every day in our home, but perhaps I've become acclimated to a daily atmosphere that surprises others when they step through the door. That delivery man is constantly going in and out of houses, and no telling what kind of spirits he has felt. He knew something was different about our home, but he couldn't identify it without help. We will be incapable of purveying peace in the congregation if we do not possess it in the parsonage.

When I was being interviewed for my application to serve as a chaplain with the Missouri State Highway Patrol, one of the lieutenants came to our house for a visit. I was impressed when he also interviewed my wife and children, then he stopped and talked to a few of the neighbors. I've often wondered why this procedure has never been implemented with those we consider licensing into a ministerial organization. Peter and Paul's pastoral epistles make it abundantly clear that the condition of a church leader's home qualifies or disqualifies him/her from leading God's house. Once again, "The children of this world are in their generation wiser than the children of light" (Luke 16:8, KJV).

Many years ago, a pastor invited me to preach to his congregation. After one evening service, I was invited to their home for a snack. They had five or six young children, and it was chaotic to say the least. I will never forget the mother standing at the cupboard and tossing paper plates, cups, forks, and knives at the kids and me, who were sitting at the table not far away. Most everything she threw at us ended up on the floor before making it to the table. The kids seemed to think it was fun, but to me it seemed chaotic and inhospitable. Was this episode a commentary on their family life? I think so. Today, none of those children are walking with God.

J. T. Pugh once said, "Whatever is in the heart of a pastor will eventually come out in the congregation." This statement keeps me humble and on my knees in prayer. It has become my habit before I speak to our congregation that I ask God to create in me a clean heart and renew in me a right spirit. During the preaching of the word, the congregation becomes highly susceptible to the speaker's spirit, and any spiritual virus, contagion, or attitude could poison the well. I've been to a few church meetings where I wish I could have pulled out a twelve-ounce aerosol can of "sweet, sweet spirit" and sprayed it everywhere.

Many years ago, I heard about an area pastor who at times verbally assaulted Pentecostal theology, particularly the biblical experience of speaking with other tongues. I was told he had written a book expressing his views about the gifts of the Spirit, so I ventured into the bookstore on their campus to investigate. I located the book and began perusing it. A female employee came over to me and asked if I had any questions. I replied, "Just one. I noticed that this book written by your pastor is academically inadequate. He quotes no sources, includes no notes, and cites no bibliography. It is also mean-spirited in that it attacks the theology of millions of other credible Christians around the world without supporting his arguments properly."

She looked at me and said, "Mean-spirited? Oh, that's him all right."

I have often conjectured that the things a person does publicly can be multiplied many times when done in private. I mark church leaders who don't treat their spouses, children, and others in the congregation or the public with kindness. People who are rude or belligerent in public are capable of much worse in private. I have also observed that speakers who take an uncharacteristically hard line on any one issue can't seem to let up, and consistently become agitated when talking about it, are usually hiding something in their own life.

The apostle Paul shared his battles with us in his writings. Despite his many stormy conflicts and dangers, he valued peace and used it as a spiritual weapon to advance the kingdom of God as well as his own spiritual vitality. Perhaps the principal reason why Paul could live his life in a climate of peace was because he was in charge of his own spirit and in touch with God. While in prison, he wrote to believers in Philippi that he couldn't seem to choose between life or death because either one was to his benefit (Phil. 1:21).

Paul demonstrated the high value his placed upon peace in Philippians 4:6–9:

> Be anxious for nothing, but in everything by prayer and supplication, with thanksgiving, let your requests be made known to God; and the peace of God, which surpasses all understanding, will guard your hearts and minds through Christ Jesus. Finally, brethren, whatever things are true, whatever things are noble, whatever things are just, whatever things are pure, whatever things are lovely, whatever things are of good report, if

> there is any virtue and if there is anything praise-
> worthy—meditate on these things. The things
> which you learned and received and heard and
> saw in me, these do, and the God of peace will
> be with you.

He identified peace as the mitigator of anxiety, the guard of his heart (emotions) and mind (thoughts), the filter for his medita-tion choices, and his constant companion. In Colossians he revealed that God rules our hearts through his peace upon us (3:15), and in Romans he wrote that the God of peace swiftly crushes Satan under our feet (16:20). I believe God has given us his authority to walk and live in peace. Occasional storms will rise to threaten our peace, such as when Jesus was asleep in the boat. The disciples fought against the storm with all of their seafaring acumen and ability, but it was not until they cried out to Jesus and placed him in charge of the storm that peace was restored.

Jesus sent out the seventy (Luke 10) and instructed them to declare peace to every house they approached. He told them that if the son of peace received them, they should stay there; if he didn't receive them, they were to shake the dust off their feet and move on. It is interesting that the meaning of "son of peace" connotes the idea of one who is worthy of such a blessing, who is peaceable and kind, and does not fight against God. Believers who are at peace with God will be at peace with other sons of peace. Jesus's implicit lesson was that the seventy should not waste their time with people who were not ready for peace.

Jesus never said, "Blessed are the peacekeepers," because it is impossible to keep peace. However, he did say, "Blessed are the peace-makers," because it usually is possible to make peace. In Romans 12:18, Paul said, "If it is possible, as much as depends on you, live peaceably with all men." It appears here that Paul is conceding that on occasion we will encounter people who refuse to live peaceably. In all other instances, however, we should make every effort to create, recover, or maintain peace.

Achieving peace produces the fruit of righteousness (Heb. 12:11). This being the case, I think we can conclude that manifesting *un*righteousness is the fruit produced by a lack of peace. Hebrews 12:14 says, "Pursue peace with all people, and holiness, without which no one will see the Lord." This tells me that living in peace and reaching for peace apparently makes it a holiness issue. In other words, if we are "sons of peace," we will present Christ to everyone around us, and we will one day see the Prince of Peace face to face. Verse 11 assures that when peace is restored, it will once again produce the peaceable fruit of righteousness.

I try to keep all of my relationship accounts short. My default response is to place everyone in the "best possible motive" column. This keeps my mind free from the peace robbers of suspicion and doubt. I love to make peace, and as far as I know, I do not have an enemy in the world. There is nothing quite like reestablishing peace where there once was division.

Paul informed the believers at Rome that "the kingdom of God is not eating and drinking, but righteousness and peace and joy in the Holy Spirit" (Rom. 14:17). Thus one-third of the primary dynamics at work within the kingdom of God is peace, and all three operate through the Holy Spirit.

> Now may the God of peace who brought up our Lord Jesus from the dead, that great Shepherd of the sheep, through the blood of the everlasting covenant, make you complete in every good work to do His will, working in you what is well pleasing in His sight, through Jesus Christ, to whom be glory forever and ever. Amen. (Heb. 13:20–21)

CHAPTER 8

CHRISTLIKE LEADERS
PASS THE HURT TEST

> *So Jesus said, "Are you also still without understanding? Do you not yet understand that whatever enters the mouth goes into the stomach and is eliminated? But those things which proceed out of the mouth come from the heart, and they defile a man. For out of the heart proceed evil thoughts, murders, adulteries, fornications, thefts, false witness, blasphemies. These are the things which defile a man, but to eat with unwashed hands does not defile a man" (Matthew 15:16–20).*

"Eighty and six years have I served Him,
and yet he has done me no wrong."—Polycarp

Jesus explained a powerful principle for all believers, but particularly for those in leadership, when he said it is not what goes into a man that defiles him but rather what comes out of him. How we process crushing events, fiery trials, and difficult people will expose what we are made of. Just because something happens to us does not mean it must have a negative effect within us. It doesn't have to end up in defilement. My dad often said, "God decides what we go through, but we decide how we will go through it."

Fiery trials effect different things within different people. It has been said that the sun melts wax and hardens clay. What makes the difference is the composition of the material under the heat of the sun. Fire will temper leaders, help them understand where the people they are leading are living, burn away arrogance, and advance growth and development.

Life has a way of throwing people into the fire. If you have been through the fire, you can typically discern within a few minutes whether or not the person you are listening to has been through fire. When Shadrach, Meshach, and Abednego came out of the fiery furnace, the scripture says their bands were burned away and they did not smell like smoke. Paul said that fire reveals the materials we have used to build our life: wood, hay, stubble or gold, silver, and precious stones (1 Cor. 3:12). If you have built your life with inferior materials, the fire will burn you up and you will not last. If you have built your life with precious materials (gold, silver, and jewels) the fire will only purge and perfect you.

What is the prerequisite for fire burning you better rather than burning you up? First, you must recognize when you are on fire. We live in the Midwest where we enjoy four seasons. Every fall we buy firewood to burn off the chill on cold nights, although our fireplace is more for entertainment than to ease our gas bill. I like bringing wood into the house, positioning the logs, and setting the log lighter. I enjoy the woodsy smell and the snap, crackle, and pop of a roaring fire.

Toward the end of winter a few years ago, a small pile of logs was still cluttering up my wood storage area. I gathered them up, tossed them in the fireplace, and set the log lighter. I was enjoying my masterpiece fire when Marlene suddenly noticed an unusual roar in our chimney. It sounded like a jet during takeoff. She ran out the front door and saw that the top of our chimney looked like the Fourth of July as sparks came flying out of our flue, spangling the evening sky.

We called 911, and within minutes a huge pumper firetruck lumbered onto our street. The shooting sparks and noise of the firetruck attracted a small crowd of concerned neighbors. By that time, we had managed to put the fire out, but we were still a little shaken. The fire chief determined that the fire started because I had failed to have our chimney periodically cleaned of carcinogenic buildup. After a kind lecture, the firefighters gathered up the embers, dumped them in a snowbank, and drove off.

We waited until warmer weather arrived and then had the chimney repaired. My three-year-old granddaughter, Melina, was intrigued with the fact Papa's house was torn up. My son Justin explained to her what I had done, and for months she retold the story of "Papa burned the chimney down!" I have often wondered what would have happened had my wife not recognized that our house was on fire.

The Holy Spirit is likened unto fire in scripture. When fire is burning in a suitable place, it provides heat, energy, light, and incineration. When fire is not managed, of course it is immensely destructive. Fortunately, what the enemy means for evil God can convert into something good. We must recognize when we are on fire and take immediate measures to control it for our good.

Just this morning I spoke with a licensed minister who is going through the fire. He broke down sobbing several times on the phone, explaining that he and his wife are going to different churches. He just spent a week in the hospital battling serious diabetic issues (doctors had to amputate a toe). He now has major medical bills, and their refinancing application has been denied. He is so overweight that he can't find clothes suitable for church. His teenage daughter is separated from her newlywed husband, and they are both seeing other people while they are legally married.

Thus the question is not "Am I going to be hurt?" because you *are* going to be hurt. The right question is what are you going to do with the hurt? Are you going to become angry, bitter, or receive offense into your spirit? Or are you going to pray, stay humble, seek God, forgive, and walk the high road?

As previously mentioned, I was elected to my first pastorate at age twenty-five. I was four years out of Bible college and had been married four years. I had served as a youth pastor for three years and evangelized for one year. My wife and I had an infant son. There is no question this church took a chance on an unknown like me. Anyone can be elected as the pastor of a church in one business meeting, but it takes quite some time to become more than a pastor in title. Just because someone holds the position doesn't mean they are the leader.

I figured out during the first board meeting that I was not the leader in the room. They may have called me pastor, but I was not in charge. Anytime I made a suggestion to the church board, I noticed that everyone's eyes swiveled toward one man in the room—and it wasn't me. If he was smiling and nodding, the suggestion would go through; if he was frowning and looking down, it would crash.

However, I was wise enough to figure out that if I could at least influence the leader, then perhaps I could still accomplish my agenda. Unfortunately, there was no pleasing him. One of the many lessons I learned about leadership in that dynamic was not to take my disappointment to the platform. I learned what it was like to preach about the warm blood of Calvary to icy stares and folded arms. I experienced the pain of having a meeting called by the board to have me dismissed as pastor. Though the heat of the fire was intense, that congregation never saw me sweat.

I decided I would not let someone else choose my attitude as a leader. I decided I would not create a bully pulpit and preach out of my pain or frustration. I decided I would do everything I could to keep a good spirit and lead that small congregation into revival and growth.

For two years prior to our arrival, no one had stepped into the baptistery, and it had become a storage bin. So one Saturday I went to the church and cleared it out, cleaned it up, filled it with water, and started the heater. Someone came in and demanded, "What do you think you're doing?"

I said, "Well, just maybe, someone might want to be baptized today. After all, isn't that our mission?"

God helped us to baptized sixteen people in our first three months, and the church started to grow. I naively thought everyone would be excited and begin to participate in the mission. Wrong! All hades broke loose. One man accused me of compromising the doctrine because he didn't see any of those new people repenting at the altar. I explained to him they had already repented at their kitchen table after a Bible study.

Another man complained that all the new little kids were smearing their dirty hands on the freshly painted walls of the Sunday school classroom. Others pointed out that I didn't have a "real job." Someone questioned whether I had a genuine call to preach. Eventually, the board reduced my salary, so I took a job selling *USA Today* newspapers just to pay bills. One Saturday night at a church business meeting, total chaos erupted. People stood up and shouted at each other and at me. Ugly human spirits were exposed. After the meeting, I told my wife to drive our infant son home because I felt the walk home would do me good. I cried every step of the way, discouraged, despondent, not knowing what to do. At home I told Marlene, "No one's going to show up for church tomorrow morning." We felt they all hated each other and us.

I called my district superintendent for advice. After hearing my story, he advised me to terminate the church board, but I felt I couldn't do that. I was concerned that the church would split and souls would be lost. I felt my only recourse was to keep a good spirit and wait on God. Through all of this I learned a valuable lesson—be patient. It is God's church, and when he does something, he does it right.

I had expected that my family would be the only attendees the next morning, but when church time came, there they all were, ensconced in their assigned seats in the pews, sanctimonious expressions intact. At the end of my uninspired message, I did something I had never done there before: I asked if anyone had a good word to say for the Lord. One elderly man, who had been attending for about a year, struggled to his feet. I had been told that he and his wife had not been attending another church of our faith for about eight years, and he had not been present the night before at the fateful business meeting. Up until that moment he had hardly moved a muscle or said a word to anyone in the church, so when he stood up, all heads turned and all eyes focused on him.

This man was six feet four inches tall and weighed over three hundred pounds. He looked up at the pulpit, pointed his finger at me, and declared, "Church, that young man is my pastor. Whatever he tells me to do, I will do it with all my heart. If he tells me to go over to that corner and stand on my head, I may die trying, but at least I'm going to try." Suddenly, he lifted his hands and began to worship God. The presence of God fell upon him and he began to speak with tongues. Despite the fact that he was close to seventy and overweight, he took off shuffling down the aisle, praising God.

I was amazed at what happened next. Several people began to worship. The Holy Spirit began to move. Some prayed; others were respectful and quiet. It truly was a breakthrough. Over the next two years many changes evolved. Several board members resigned, new people came (blessed additions), and we had a few funerals (blessed subtractions), but the Lord blessed and the attendance nearly doubled.

I have to say there were many good people in that congregation who wanted to grow spiritually and who wanted to support us, but they were not in the control group. We have maintained a good long-distance relationship with these few through the years. After we resigned and moved away, we later returned to the area to speak at a meeting nearby. When I arrived, I was told that the elder who had resisted our leadership had been diagnosed with terminal cancer.

I called him on the phone. When he heard my voice, he interrupted and said, "Oh, Pastor Gleason, thank you for calling. You know, since my diagnosis I've been doing some thinking. Some of the things I used to think were so important are now not important at all." I think this was his attempt at apologizing for all the heartache he had caused. Before hanging up, we laughed, we cried, we forgave, and we prayed together. He passed two months later.

Today, that church is a thriving congregation enjoying a multimillion-dollar campus. I have been invited back more than once to speak. I am so thankful the Lord sent me there. It was a place to learn, to grow, to succeed and fail, but at least God helped us to fail forward. It was during that season that I learned to take my troubles to God in prayer and not air them in frustration from the platform. Many nights I wept in the presence of God, sometimes feeling sorry for myself, but most of the time trying to become acquainted with Jesus in the fellowship of his suffering (Philippians 3:10).

During those five years trying to pastor a small family-owned-and-operated congregation, I became fluent in Robert's Rules of Order. I learned how to respond to attacks with grace and diplomacy. I learned how to protect new believers from the "us-four-and-no-more" establishment. I learned how resilient the body of Christ really is, and how the people of God are able to respond when they believe in the integrity of leadership. One man told me, "I rarely agree with you, but I know your heart is always in the right place."

I occasionally chuckle or wince when I hear pastors complain about their congregation. Their critiques may range from complaining about the people's pitiful giving, bad attitudes, or tepid worship, to dead heads in the pew, new-convert killers, or preacher haters. One long-term evangelist and short-term pastor jokingly remarked, "The only thing I miss about pastoring is those little yellow envelopes."

Some leaders like to blame their church trouble on someone or something else and are reluctant to take ownership of the culture they have created. They may find it convenient to impugn their predecessor or point to the power center within the congregation or the devil as the culprit of the confusion. The truth is, if they have served that congregation for at least a few years, they can blame no one else but themselves for their troubles. This does not mean they are responsible for every sin and disobedient act committed by members of the church. There is a big difference between individuals in a church with troubles and church trouble.

Have you passed the hurt test? It could be the next step to your promotion by God. It could also be the reason you haven't yet been promoted. I watched as my father successfully passed the hurt test. Those that hurt him eventually lost influence, but God continued to give him great honor and promotion until the day he died. The grindstone of life will either grind us down or polish us up. We can choose to be stumbling blocks or stepping stones for those who follow us.

It has been said you can't keep a good man down. I would add that you can't keep a bad man up. If you pass the hurt test, God has greater things in store for you. If you fail the hurt test, your future will be very limited. The people we serve deserve leadership without the smell of smoke on their spirit. Bitterness is an acid that destroys its container, but forgiveness is an ointment that heals everything it touches.

CHAPTER 9

CHRISTLIKE LEADERS GIVE THE GIFT OF GREATNESS

But Jesus called them to Himself and said to them, "You know that those who are considered rulers over the Gentiles lord it over them, and their great ones exercise authority over them. Yet it shall not be so among you; but whoever desires to become great among you shall be your servant (Mark 10:42–43).

"It is one of the most beautiful compensations of this life that no man can sincerely try to help another without helping himself."—Ralph Waldo Emerson

C an we be great? Is it appropriate to talk about greatness or to reach for greatness in the kingdom of God? Conversations about greatness typically do not exist in most circles of Christianity. We don't hear pastors or church leaders talk about becoming great lest we attract the judgment of God due to pride and arrogance. We are well versed in scriptural references to pride and humility. We know that God resists the proud but gives grace to the humble (1 Peter 5:5).

Before I attempt to position greatness with Jesus and his followers, let me first visit humility. Some people have to work really hard at obtaining humility, but for others it comes naturally. Bottom line, some have it, some don't. For the life of me I don't understand why some are not humbler than they are because "they are arrogant for no apparent reason," as my father-in-law used to say. My dad used to quip about an author who announced the release of his new book, *My Humility and How I Obtained It*.

A small group of leaders from several congregations had gathered to elect officials. Among them was a minister who desperately desired to be elected to a position—any position—among his colleagues. The first office to fill was that of sectional presbyter. Among the dozen or so voters, there were four names on the nominating ballot, and the first three withdrew their names from consideration. The fourth name was the man who craved a position. He had received one vote (presumably his own) and was the last man standing. The voters were directed to ratify him with a voice vote. Upon his ratification he was invited to the platform to accept his election. He walked slowly and stately, savoring his life's crowning moment. He dramatically placed his hands on the outside edges of the pulpit and hung his head in presumed humility. After a dramatic pause, he slowly looked up and said, "Gentlemen, thank you for your vote of confidence."

In some cases, especially this one, we can mistake arrogance for naivety. This man clearly was a misguided title-seeking novice. His passion to be a big duck in a little pond is disappointing. Somewhere along his journey he had absorbed some wrong ideas and perspectives. Church business situations like these usually do not turn out well. I never like to see someone actually get the job they crave so desperately. My observation is that the people who are not seeking positions do a much better job with them than people who are. Some leaders are changed by the acquisition of power while others are unaffected by the sudden gain or loss of it. When a leader is bigger than the job, he will change the job; when the job is bigger than he, it will change him, and usually not for the better.

I realize that in Christian circles the subject of becoming great is taboo, but Jesus didn't have a problem with his disciples talking about or reaching for greatness. In fact, he was the one who introduced the subject of greatness to his disciples. Why not talk about greatness? His goal for the disciples certainly was not for them to become lousy!

In 1978 I graduated from a small Bible college in St. Paul, Minnesota. The college shared a campus with my local church, and my pastor was a member of the faculty. I served as the president of my class, graduated with honors, and got engaged graduation weekend with a November wedding in view. That summer my pastor asked me to give him a ride home from an activity involving both of us. We lived in the same neighborhood, and I was proud to provide this service to him. As we rode along, he asked me what my plans were now that I had graduated. I replied, "I'm going to enter full-time ministry as an itinerant youth speaker." I could say this with a certain degree of confidence because I had contacted a pastor from Illinois who was a young preacher's friend. Earlier that year he had offered to line up some meetings for me in his area. He had managed to secure eight consecutive youth events beginning in February.

I was excited about this opportunity. Having eight consecutive weeks booked in my calendar felt like eternal security for this start-up speaker. It hadn't yet occurred to me what might happen when that was over. My pastor had offered me no official position, so I followed his philosophy of walking through the door God had opened. I anticipated he would be excited about my plans, pat me on the back, and give me a big "atta-boy." Was I ever wrong. He sighed, looked at me, and said, "Well, Stan, I will hate seeing you spread your mediocrity all over the country." I must admit I was unprepared for that ringing endorsement. With that, I pulled into his driveway, and he got out of the car. Now forty-two years later I'm still spreading my mediocrity all over the country, this time with ink and paper.

James and John approached Jesus about achieving greatness in his kingdom. Their mother chimed in by taking Jesus aside and requesting important positions for her sons. Had this family ever discussed this subject, or were they simply highly motivated people? Think of all the responses Jesus could have given for their request: he could have rebuked them for their selfish desire and carnal ambition, he could have used this as a talking point to dumb down their future expectations as his followers, or he could have launched a rant about why greatness is self-serving and mediocrity should be our goal.

In fact, Jesus was not disappointed by their quest for greatness. His goal for them was certainly not to become mired in mediocrity. His problem with the sons of thunder and their mother was not their desire to reach for greatness but rather which path would they follow to achieve it: his path or the world's path? He informed them that there was a cup of sacrifice they must be willing to drink. They assured him they were prepared to drink it, and they eventually did. I assume you've already heard the lecture "Be Great in the Kingdom of God by Humbling Yourself and Serving Others." I assume you are practicing this Jesus model of servant-leadership. But this chapter is not about that.

Typically, we think of humility as the absence of arrogance, pridefulness, or presumption; the willingness to take a back seat, keep it low key, and avoid self-promotion. But there are more ways of humbling oneself than just these. The powerful expression of humility is also the path to greatness for church leaders (or anyone), and *that path is to prefer others more than oneself.* This is counterintuitive to the carnal mind, but it works every time it is tried in God's kingdom.

Notice how Jesus practiced giving the gift of greatness throughout his short ministry. To begin, consider how he personally employed the economy of the kingdom. At times Jesus operated in all seven spiritual gifts recorded in Romans 12:4–8: prophet, server, teacher, exhorter, giver, leader, or dispenser of compassion. If you had to choose his dominant gift, which would it be? I think if you synthesized all four Gospels, you would conclude that Jesus most often demonstrated his gift as teacher (rabbi). This is a significant discovery within the context of this chapter: "Christlike Leaders Give the Gift of Greatness."

Dr. C. Peter Wagner indicated that the spiritual gift of "teacher" is the special God-given ability to communicate information relevant to the health and ministry of the body of Christ in such a way that others will learn.[13] Called and gifted teachers have certain similar traits: they love to spend large amounts of time in study, working hard on details, and organizing their thoughts. They search for illustrations that will connect the material to the students. Gifted teachers spend time with their students and welcome questions. They are careful not to manipulate or intimidate their learning culture. They are not threatened or defensive when criticized.

Perhaps most significant, a called and gifted teacher loves to see his/her students grow—but there's more. Not only do they want them to grow, they will position their students for success so that *their students will exceed them*. But wait, there's still more: called teachers will *celebrate* the success of their students, even if/when they excel beyond whatever they themselves have achieved. This is what I call "giving the gift of greatness."

The attitude of Jesus the teacher (rabbi) is embodied in his words to the disciples in John 14:12: "Most assuredly, I say to you, he who believes in Me, the works that I do he will do also; and greater works than these he will do, because I go to My Father."

Let's draw some conclusions from Jesus's remarkable statement: First, we know that Jesus's disciples believed in him, but we also know Jesus believed in his disciples. Too many church leaders want their followers to believe in them, but they somehow don't understand that what their followers need most is for someone to believe in them. It's a wonderful thing when the church believes in the pastor; it's even more wonderful when the pastor believes in the church.

Second, Jesus did not make a superstar out of himself. He was not a one-way-street leader with everything going his way. He believed in his team, and he shared his life, ministry, and success with them. He told them they soon would be doing the same things he had been doing. Great leaders understand that most of what they do

---

[13] C. Peter Wagner, *Your Spiritual Gifts Can Help Your Church Grow* (Ventura, CA: Regal Books, 1979), 127.

can be done by others, so why not share ministry responsibility with the team? Of course, there were some things that only Jesus could do, namely, be God. Therefore, great leaders do what only they can do, then they share everything else with their team.

Third, Jesus prophesied that his team members would exceed him. Please don't miss this because we are breathing rare air in this moment. How many church leaders want to see their protégés do more and better than they? Unhealthy leaders have a need to be needed and therefore cannot celebrate the success of their subjects. Christ believed in his followers and pictured a future that outshone his own ministry on earth. He truly gave them the gift of greatness; he gave them permission to become great in his kingdom.

Embedded in some church cultures is the perception that if the leader gives something away, the leader himself is depleted. We could relate this to the "zero-sum balance" equation, or the idea that each participant's gain or loss is exactly balanced by the losses or gains of the other participants. If the total gains of the participants are added up and the total losses are subtracted, they will sum to zero.

For example, if there is a chocolate cake in the room, and you get a slice of it, then that is one less slice for me. The notion that God's blessings on you leave less blessings for me is absurd, yet some persist in leading people this way. This ideology is simply not true in the kingdom of God. We don't have just one cake; we are a cake factory. Your success does not deplete mine nor does my success deplete yours.

God is not a socialist. To illustrate, notice how Jesus presented a parable in Matthew 25. The parable goes that a master distributed talents to his servants—five, two, and one respectively. The servants with five and two talents invested and doubled their leader's resources. The servant with one talent did nothing with it. When the master returned, he celebrated and rewarded the first two servants, but he took the one talent from the slothful servant and gave it to one who had proven his/her faithfulness. God does not equalize his church by diminishing the faithful and rewarding the slothful. He rewards the faithful who are in covenant relationship with him, but the disobedient are on their own.

Finally, Jesus equipped, empowered, and celebrated his followers, then he told them he was leaving them. This is remarkable. After
only forty-two months of training, he was going to turn his entire
life's work over to his team. He was confident that he had done an
efficient job of preparing them for success, and he did not need to
hang around and look over their shoulders.

I have been around leaders who did not embrace this Christlike
attitude. If someone else's light began shining more brightly than
theirs, they hit the dimmer switch. I heard about one pastor who
hired a new assistant and immediately marched him out to the platform, where he took a piece of chalk and drew a semicircle on the
carpet in the space where the speaker would stand at the pulpit. Then
he sternly warned, "Do not step into my space!" That assistant should
have resigned on the spot because no turf protector has the ability to
build greatness in people.

Jesus did not draw circles around pseudo sacred places and
spout idle threats at potential offenders should they violate his space.
He never said, "Don't stand in my pulpit, don't sit in my chair, don't
park in my spot, and don't steal my show." Jesus did not spend his
ministry time acquiring position, power, and prestige; he spent his
life giving away everything he had. It is staggering to consider all he
could have done for himself using his absolute power. But everything
Jesus had he shared or released to others. He gave his time to his disciples, his virtue to a woman with a health issue, his healing touch to
the lepers, his protection to an adulterous woman, his prayer room
to his betrayer, his rights to his accusers, his back to the tormentors,
his hands and feet to the executioners, his power and authority to his
earth-partners, and his eternal destination to his covenant children.

In Acts 6, the apostles followed the lead of their rabbi when
they were confronted with a crisis: racism had raised its ugly head
in this fledgling Jerusalem church. Greek widows were complaining over perceived preferential treatment on behalf of their Hebrew
counterparts. What would the apostles do? Would they exert control, dominate the scene, pull on the reins, circle the wagons? No!
They had studied Jesus and knew his methods. They did exactly as
he would have done: they informed the church that they would not

trade what only they could do for what others were qualified to do. Seven men were then appointed to serve this need while the apostles gave themselves to prayer and the ministry of the Word. The result was that this decision "pleased the whole multitude" (perhaps this is the only time in church history where this happened?).

The results of these first church leaders decentralizing the congregation are staggering: "Then the word of God spread, and the number of the disciples multiplied greatly in Jerusalem, and a great many of the priests were obedient to the faith" (Acts 6:7). Any time we give our power away to qualified people around us, the results will be positive. The apostles laid their hands on these seven men and ordained them to wait on tables. Of course, we know they soon were destined for more than just appeasing crabby widows. Stephen worked miracles in the streets among the people, and Philip soon witnessed miracles in Samaria. He cast out devils, healed the sick, and baptized enough believers to fill the entire city with joy (Acts 8:8).

The question is not "Will the ministry work get done?" but rather, "Who will the leader(s) allow to do the ministry?" The average-size church in America is seventy-five members. Is there a reason for this ceiling? Yes: you can survive at seventy-five! There is no mystical barrier that hovers over a church, preventing it from growing once it reaches this average. The lead pastor can do most everything in a congregation of seventy-five. He can do all the preaching, teaching, counseling, service leading, hospital visitation, funerals, weddings, guest follow-up, lawn care, building maintenance, and the like. In order to exceed the average, the pastor must come to a crossroads and decide to give the gift of greatness; he must decentralize the power-center of the church in order to maximize potential.

Giving the gift of greatness essentially means to lift others above oneself. My father was one of the greatest Christians I ever knew. He trained young people for ministry as well as being a musical genius. He could get music out of just about anybody. For thirty years he led the Bible college choir, and each summer took a chorale on the road. His musical groups were often invited to sing at large conferences, storied church campgrounds, and local congregations. His choir recorded the first album of its kind in the early 1950s and subsequently recorded many albums for purchase. He was well known in our circle of Christianity by the time I graduated from the college.

Shortly before he died at the age of seventy-eight, after a five-year battle with cancer, he took me aside and said, "Son, you have exceeded me." I was stunned by his unexpected remark. I was thirty-nine and had not achieved any comparable notoriety, so I couldn't see any context for such a statement. He just quietly but assuredly spoke it over me. I didn't know what his statement meant at the time, but years later it became clear; he was giving me the gift of greatness. He did not want me to flounder in his shadow; he wanted me to succeed and reach for greatness in the kingdom of God. I am forever indebted to him for giving me his blessing and permission to excel.

I now stand on his shoulders. You also stand on the shoulders of someone great who believed in you and spoke about a bright future for your life. It has been said that the rising tide lifts all of the boats. Is your life and leadership a rising tide? Are you using your power to lift those around you? Author Steve Farber wrote that when you prefer others over yourself, you are not standing in an empty well but rather in an elevator cab. You are not lifting others at your expense; you are rising behind them. Our ceiling must become the floor of the next generation.[14]

Farber told the story of the first day of an elementary-school class. The teacher asked each student to share what they wanted to be when they grew up. The children began giving the predictable answers: airplane pilot, professional baseball, football or basketball player, doctor, lawyer, scientist, president of the United States, and such like. Finally, there was one student left who had not yet shared his dream. When she called on him to respond, she was not prepared for his answer: "I want to help everyone become what they want to be." I don't think that teacher gave an altar call at that moment, but she could have. Someone in your life needs you to give them the gift of greatness.

---

[14] Steve Farber, *Greater Than Yourself: The Ultimate Lesson of True Leadership* (New York, NY: Doubleday, 2009).

CHAPTER 10

CHRISTLIKE LEADERS FELLOWSHIP CHRIST

That I may know Him and the power of His resurrection, and the fellowship of His sufferings, being conformed to His death (Philippians 3:10).

For He shall grow up before Him as a tender plant, and as a root out of dry ground. He has no form or comeliness; and when we see Him, there is no beauty that we should desire Him. He is despised and rejected by men, a Man of sorrows and acquainted with grief. And we hid, as it were, our faces from Him; He was despised, and we did not esteem Him. Surely He has borne our griefs and carried our sorrows; yet we esteemed Him stricken, smitten by God, and afflicted (Isaiah 53:2–4).

"Every failure is a prayer failure."—Lee Stoneking

Jesus was the only flawless leader in world history. He did all things well. None of the clichés that typically describe and excuse new/ young leaders applied to him. Jesus experienced no learning curve, no on-the-job training, no trial and error, no getting it right next time, no lack of experience, no figuring it out, no all's well that ends well (which is code for "We sure did blow that early on, but somehow we miraculously finished up just fine"), and no fake it until you make it.

The day Jesus was baptized, John boldly declared, "Behold the lamb of God who takes away the sin of the world." This was no random or arbitrary statement that John plucked out of thin air for dramatic effect. This was an informed declaration. John was the son of a priest named Zacharias, who was serving in the temple the day the angel appeared and told him his wife, Elizabeth, would have a son. John was raised in the home of a man who well understood the procedure of the sacrificial lamb.

It was the sinner's lawful obligation to bring a firstling of the flock for sacrifice. The lamb was placed into the hands of the high priest, who then would carefully examine the lamb. What was he looking for? Marks, blemishes, disease, and imperfections. There were numerous blights, any one of which would immediately disqualify that lamb and require another.

It should be noted that the priest never inspected the sinner who approached the altar to offer a sacrifice. There was no need to interrogate the guilty; he only needed to examine the lamb. He knew that if the lamb was perfect, no matter what the sinner had done, the lamb was enough.

Incidentally, the lamb metaphor not only has significance within it from the Old Testament atonement procedures, but there is another less obvious attribute of the lamb; namely, the blood of a lamb provides the only chemical composition in any animal that is impervious to the venomous bite of a serpent. Chemists use lamb's blood to develop the serum that neutralizes a deadly strike. Not only is the metaphor powerful in the sense of the innocent dying for the guilty, but contained within that sacrificial lamb is the only blood that neutralizes the sting of sin.

John was Jesus's cousin. The scripture is silent regarding any prior interaction, but we can assume they had enjoyed family fellowship on numerous occasions. We manage a glimpse of the familial relationship when Mary, upon discovering her pregnancy, journeyed to her cousin Elizabeth's home to compare messianic and forerunner notes. When Mary declared, "My soul magnifies the Lord" (Magnificat), Elizabeth's baby leaped in her womb. John, being six months older, and growing up with Jesus in the family, had a front-row seat to Jesus's life, attitude, and actions that formed his reputation. John was qualified to examine this Lamb and to declare him fit and perfect for the ultimate sacrifice for humanity's sin problem.

The moment Jesus approached John at the Jordan, John fully understood his assignment. He was the only man in the world qualified to introduce the Messiah, the examined and perfect sacrifice. Like a man who was operating in his purpose, John declared, "Behold, the Lamb of God who takes away the sin of the world!" John had prepared the way for him; he had examined him thoroughly and had now approved him as the only man in the world qualified for this mission.

We don't have to be perfect leaders. Someone else has already been there and done that, and got the nail scars. But we *do* have to follow the perfect one if we desire to lead others in his enterprise, the church. The apostle Paul outlined a pretty impressive resume in Philippians 3. He informed his readers that he was "of the stock of Israel, of the tribe of Benjamin, a Hebrew of the Hebrews; concerning the law, a Pharisee; concerning zeal, persecuting the church; concerning the righteousness which is in the law, blameless" (Phil. 3:5–6)

However, he was quick to inform his audience that despite his significant qualifications by birth, education, and experience, he was still trying to attain the fullness of Christ. After thirty years of walking with Jesus, breaking into continents and cities with the gospel, writing scripture, ascending into the third heaven, and developing over a dozen of his own disciples who were now elders, the apostle Paul acknowledged that he was still reaching to be like Jesus. Church leaders should pay close attention to Paul's pursuit of Jesus Christ.

Paul provided insight into his inner passion to pursue Christ: "I don't mean to say that I have already achieved these things or that I have already reached perfection. But I press on to possess that perfection for which Christ Jesus first possessed me" (Phil. 3:12, NLT). It appears Paul was saying that after all his years of experience, he did not count himself as one who had made it, but rather he was still trying to get up to Christlike speed and get ahold of the one who had got ahold of him.

A father may take his young daughter by the hand and lead her safely across a busy street. He may instruct her to hold tightly to his hand and stay close to him. She may feel that because of her tight grip she is going to be safe. But the truth is that her father understands he must be the one to look both ways, and he has a much stronger grip on her than she has on him. If she makes it, it will be due much more to his grip than hers. God's grip of grace upon us is much greater than our grip of commitment on him.

When I was around eight years old my family went on vacation, traveling from Minnesota to Oregon to visit my maternal grandparents. After arriving at their house my mother's youngest brother came by on his motorcycle to see us. He must have noticed me admiring his machine because he asked if I wanted to ride it. Grinning, I quickly climbed aboard. Neither of us was wearing a helmet, and the wind whipped through out hair like we were going one hundred miles per hour. I was deliciously scared. I do not remember saying it, but after our ride, my uncle had a good time informing my parents that somewhere on the road I had confidently told him, "Okay, Uncle Frank. You can jump off now and let me take it from here."

I'm concerned that some church leaders have told God where he can get off so they "can take it from here." The truth is we are functioning in a spiritual kingdom, and there is no place to continue in flawed flesh what was begun in the Spirit. The grace of God offers more than his unmerited favor and salvation; grace is God's agent at work within us. Paul said in Philippians 2:13 that God is working in us by giving us the desire to do what he wants us to do, and then giving us the power to do it. We must not throw grace from the ride we are on, declaring that we can "take it from here." The grace it takes to save us is the grace it takes to keep us going. Any church leader who tries to lead God's people through the sheer power of their human ability will come to the end of their resources. The only possible result will be a broken leadership model and a trail of bodies.

There is no mile marker on Isaiah's "highway of holiness" where we can declare we will "take it from here." Paul employed Greek Olympic-training language when he said, "I press toward the goal for the prize of the upward call of God in Christ Jesus" (Phil. 3:14). He was analogizing his pursuit of Christ as a well-trained athlete who is straining with every developed muscle to cross the finish line, and that finish line is Jesus Christ. Jesus should be the goal in our pursuit of all ministry, all leadership, all relationships, and all holiness. Any other perceived finish line is not *the* finish line, because it falls far short of the goal. Paul said we are unwise when we compare ourselves by ourselves. If my goal is to outlead or outholy or outperform someone else, then I will never reach my full potential in Christ.

In Christ's leadership culture there was no demand or expectation for perfection. Jesus was perfect and he knew it, but not in the sense that some leaders perceive their own perfection. I have observed some church leaders who, by their attitude and actions, estimated their role as being perfected and therefore were unteachable, and they wouldn't share their ministry by developing others around them.

I occasionally tell my team—and even the congregation I serve—that I am not their goal. Neither am I afraid to admit that my life is not perfect. I have often observed the hurt of aspiring congregants who desired to excel, but knowing their weakness, gave up because their leader projected perfection upon them. If they only knew. The greatest need in leading today is to keep it real. If it's not real, it won't help anyone. The last thing a congregation needs is leaders who attempt to veil their faces, much like Moses, to hide the fading glory.

A sideline critic once accused me of being a cult leader. I laughed and replied, "I know for a fact I'm not a cult leader because nobody around here does anything I tell them to do." I have continually invited my leadership team and congregation to examine my life because I have nothing to hide. However, I am quick to warn them that if they look closely enough, they are sure to discover something that may disappoint them. That being said, it would be inappropriate for a leader to take transparency to the point of airing their proverbial dirty laundry. But our followers are energized when they know we are in the race with them, striving to reach the same finish line.

I once read a sociologist's observation of human nature. His team studied joggers in a park. When no one was looking, the joggers lollygagged along. However, when they approached observers, they picked up the pace. This same team observed sprinters in competition. They were all timed at one hundred yards multiple times. Unbeknownst to them, however, for one of their dashes the finish line was set just a little bit further than before, although they were still timed at one hundred yards. Remarkably, all of the runners improved their performance as they strained for something further.

The writer of Hebrews apparently understood what happens to the performances of competing athletes when they are being observed:

> Therefore we also, since we are surrounded by so great a cloud of witnesses, let us lay aside every weight, and the sin which so easily ensnares us, and let us run with endurance the race that is set before us, looking unto Jesus, the author and finisher of our faith, who for the joy that was set before Him endured the cross, despising the shame, and has sat down at the right hand of the throne of God. (Heb. 12:1–2)

Hebrews 11 is heralded and revered as God's hall of faith. All of the named champions of the faith ran their race well, and their exploits inspire us yet today. A cursory view of their lives may make them appear as the untouchables. Abraham was the father of the faithful and the friend of God. Jacob had the blessing and the birthright of his father, Isaac. David was the man after God's own heart. Noah found grace in the eyes of the Lord and built a magnificent water-worthy vessel to the saving of his family. Samson singlehandedly conquered thousands of the enemies of God's people. Gideon's army of three hundred defeated the formidable Midianites.

If we take a closer look at these heroes of our faith, however, we may find a few flops, fumbles, and failures. Abraham lied about his relationship to Sarah and had sex with her maid. Jacob was a deceiver and couldn't achieve anything honestly. David committed adultery, embarrassing God and all Israel, and then arranged the certain death of his lover's husband. Samson consorted with harlots. Gideon was afraid of his own shadow and was hiding in a winepress when God called him a mighty man of valor. Noah built an ark, but then he planted a vineyard and got drunk. Don't be too hard on old Noah, though. Keep in mind this unfortunate episode occurred after a building program. I can't excuse his action, but having gone through a harrowing building program once myself, I can understand it.

Perhaps this is what inspired the writer of Hebrews to quickly shift our focus from the heroes of the faith in chapter 11 to the author and the finisher of our faith in the next chapter. He wrote, "Looking unto Jesus…" It was as if he were saying, "You can glance at these heroes, but don't look too long or too close because there's baggage there. But you can gaze all you want and as closely as you want at Jesus. He is the finish line." I love this about the Bible. God's word, written by the inspiration of God, keeps it real. All of this tells us Jesus Christ is not looking for perfection in church leaders, but he does require that we make our goal a lifelong pursuit of the nature, the spirit, and the character of Jesus.

When Jesus gave the invitation to "Follow me" (Matt. 9:9), did he mean in theory or in a general way? I think not. When Jesus invited his disciples to follow him, he was saying, "Act like me, speak like me, present yourselves like me, treat others like me, and lead like me." Elder Johnny James said, "If it's not about Jesus, it's not about anything." How good of a job did Jesus do in training and expecting his disciples to lead like him? When Peter and John were called in question because of the healing of the lame man at the Gate Beautiful, their accusers recognized they had been with Jesus (Acts 4:13). The rulers, elders, and scribes had finally succeeded in getting rid of Jesus, but here were two more just like him!

The greatest compliment any believer could receive is for someone to say when they are near them that they feel and see Jesus. This was literally happening in the life of the apostle Paul. His lifelong quest was to "apprehend" Christ. What does this mean if it doesn't mean to be like him? In nearly the same stroke of the pen, Paul also wrote, "That I might know him." This is a remarkable pursuit. On the surface, it doesn't make sense: "Know him?" I would like to ask Paul, "Didn't you meet him on the road to Damascus? Were you not baptized in his name and filled with his Spirit? Didn't you behold a personal appearance of the Lord while in the Arabian desert? Haven't you been praying to him, walking with him, and laboring for him the last thirty years?"

Paul was revealing his passion to know Jesus Christ in every conceivable manner, and to imitate him in every way possible. He told us exactly how he wanted to know Jesus: "That I may know Him and the power of His resurrection, and the fellowship of His sufferings, being conformed to His death" (Phil. 3:10). Most everyone would like to know Jesus in the first way described by Paul. Who wouldn't want to experience and see a demonstration of the resurrection power of Jesus Christ? Perhaps, though, we are not as eager to sign up for the second way to know Jesus, "the fellowship of His suffering." My philosophy has always been, "No pain? Hey, no pain!" But a painless Christianity does not know Jesus intimately.

The only way to fellowship Jesus intimately is through suffering. You don't have to go looking for it; suffering will find you. As previously stated, the question is not "Are you going to be hurt?" The question is "What will you do with that hurt?" Will you plan to retaliate? To get your pound of revenge? To live angry the rest of your life? To give someone the silent treatment? These reactions make the flesh feel good, at least temporarily, but they ultimately are a waste of valuable opportunities to know Jesus more intimately.

Isaiah saw Messiah as a man of sorrows and acquainted with grief. An elder told me that one night he was praying through some personal pain, bemoaning the fact that people had told lies about him. The Lord interrupted, "I thought you said you wanted to be like me."

Taken aback, he said, "Yes, Lord, you know I want to be like you."

The Lord said, "How could you be any more like me than you are when people are lying about you and betraying you?"

After a weighty pause, the elder meekly said, "Yes, Lord."

The best response to being mistreated is not to take it to social media and rally all your friends to your side. This will not fellowship Jesus, but it may fellowship someone or something else. Take your pain to the prayer room and pour it out to Jesus. Tell him exactly what happened and how it made you feel. He can handle it. If you're angry with him for allowing it to happen, he can handle that too. What you'll eventually discover is that during that season of brokenness, even a prolonged time of weeping in his presence, something beautiful will happen; you will begin to know him in the fellowship of his suffering. When you arise from that encounter, you will be more like him than ever before.

Hurt may be perceived as injustice, but it is more like a test. Promotion is of the Lord (Ps. 75:6–7), but we don't get promoted until we pass the hurt test. When we process hurt and pain through prayer and forgiveness, we are demonstrating that we can be trusted by God to lead others. I will not unpack the story of Joseph, but because he passed the hurt test, God could trust him with power. Consequently, his new position saved his family from famine as well as preserving the messianic bloodline. The tables were turned; the bigger picture had now become clear. Joseph told his brothers: "But as for you, you meant evil against me; but God meant it for good, in order to bring it about as it is this day, to save many people alive" (Gen. 50:20).

It should be noted that Joseph is an Old Testament type of Jesus Christ with numerous striking parallels, not the least of which are (1) favored son, (2) hated and rejected by his own brethren, (3) betrayed, (4) sold into slavery, and (5) revealed to his brethren. Of all the characters rehearsed in the Old Testament, perhaps Joseph rises above them all because of the amount of text dedicated to his story (thirteen chapters), yet not one disparaging word is spoken of him. He did all things well.

For some thirteen years Joseph was tested and progressively positioned, even when no one was watching but God. Three times in Genesis 39, the scripture says, "The Lord was with him." This remarkable descriptor was affirmed by pagans in Egypt who could not deny the favor of God upon Joseph's life. You might say that Joseph was prophetically becoming like Christ.

Paul penned an arresting statement in 2 Corinthians 4:10–12: "Always carrying about in the body the dying of the Lord Jesus, that the life of Jesus also may be manifested in our body. For we who live are always delivered to death for Jesus's sake, that the life of Jesus also may be manifested in our mortal flesh. So then death is working in us, but life in you."

It appears that Paul was saying the fatal condition of Jesus on the cross was being duplicated in his own physical body. Considering Paul's catalog of all that he suffered, including 195 scars from beatings, shipwreck, dangers, stoning, and betrayal of brethren, not to mention the stress of caring for all the churches he planted (2 Cor. 11), one can begin to understand how this metamorphosis was literally transforming his body.

I have a very close friend who for the last thirty-five years has had a remarkable ministry in various parts of India. He has ministered in our congregation many times, and I have been privileged to travel to India on many occasions to partner with his ministry. He has seen entire villages become Christ followers. He has evangelized tribal colonies where it is illegal to convert them to any religion, baptizing their tribal kings and then their entire colonies. Prior to becoming Christians, their crops were failing and their babies were dying. But after baptism, not so.

He has seen every miracle imaginable, including the dead raised. He has a PhD in theology, he spoke once at Promise Keepers, he has written many small books in effort to reach people of other religions. The last fourteen years he has baptized sixty-five thousand believers, comprised mostly of Muslims (including Taliban), Sikhs, Hindus, Buddhists, and pagan.

I have often thought and publicly said he is the closest thing to Jesus my eyes have ever beheld in this world. He is humble, thankful, articulate, passionate, thoughtful, and a devoted husband, father, and grandfather. He has been beaten numerous times, and more than once left to die. He often has been endangered, suffered financial hardship, faced armed and angry men, and made many personal sacrifices for Christ's sake. Any offering I have given him has been immediately shared with his national pastors who live very meagerly.

He told me a story one day about a missionary who had come from Europe to present the gospel to a village in India. The missionary was up in years but had labored in that community as sincerely as he could. After a few unproductive years, the mother church called him to come home because he had made no disciples. He felt like a failure. As his replacement, they sent a young and aggressive but inexperienced missionary. This young man hit the ground running, preaching Jesus in the streets and anywhere people would listen. He told them that Jesus was kind and good, he loved everyone, and he was a servant.

After several months, a village elder took the young man aside and said, "You are preaching to us about Jesus? We know Jesus. He was here with us for years just before you arrived. We want you to leave and send Jesus back to us." The young missionary contacted the parent organization and told them what had happened. They called him back home and the elder missionary returned to the village and happily made many disciples for Christ.

What do you see when you look in the mirror? Is it a likeness of Christ? A long look in the mirror is good for all of us now and then. I'm not talking about the kind of look that happens first thing in the morning when you're combing your hair or brushing your teeth; I mean a good hard look at yourself. I woke up one morning and stared at myself for a moment. I didn't like what I saw: messy hair, sleepy countenance, rumpled pajamas, hunched over…and then, I smiled. Instantly there was a 10 percent improvement, which isn't saying much.

This may sound condescending—even as I write, I'm squirming—so please forgive me in advance. But are we seeing Jesus when we look in the mirror? Are we taking the personal formation of the leadership model of Jesus Christ seriously enough? Paul had deep concerns about what was forming in the believers at Galatia. He wrote, "My little children, for whom I labor in birth again until Christ is formed in you, I would like to be present with you now and to change my tone; for I have doubts about you" (Gal. 4:19–20).

How is your Christ formation? We have all witnessed deformed Christianity. My heart breaks for people like these, and for those who have been negatively impacted by them. Paul was so concerned about the dysfunction in the Galatian church that he felt the need to take them back to the birth center and have a do-over.

At the All-Indian Congress in 1927, Mahatma Gandhi reportedly said, "I like your Christ, but not your Christianity." According to scripture, we are not autonomous franchises that may take creative liberties to determine the model we will follow or become. Perhaps someone reading this is arguing with me that it is impossible to become like Jesus because we are flawed, and therefore we should just do the best we can. I understand that Jesus was perfect and we are not, but Paul apparently didn't offer that excuse.

> Now these are the gifts Christ gave to the church: the apostles, the prophets, the evangelists, and the pastors and teachers. Their responsibility is to equip God's people to do his work and build up the church, the body of Christ. This will continue until we all come to such unity in our faith and knowledge of God's Son that we will be mature in the Lord, measuring up to the full and complete standard of Christ. (Eph. 4:10–13, NLT)

Another version reads, "This will continue until we are united by our faith and by our understanding of the Son of God. Then we will be mature, just as Christ is, and we will be completely like him" (Eph. 4:13, CEV). Paul situated the governmental ministry of the church (fivefold ministry) as the primary equippers and developers of the saints. Paul assumed that healthy, well-balanced, Christlike church leaders will equip, train, and model Christ to the point of their full maturity in Christ.

John seemed to agree when he wrote, "Love has been perfected among us in this: that we may have boldness in the day of judgment; because as He is, so are we in this world" (1 John 4:17). Apparently, we need not settle for stunted spiritual growth, but have been given permission to reach for Jesus in his full stature until we are looking eyeball to eyeball with the goal of our spiritual maturity! If you are reaching for the model of Jesus Christ, then you are qualified to lead others.

I made an amazing discovery many years ago. Every time I have paid attention to this revelation and honored it, I have been pleased, and every time I have ignored it, it has come back to bite me. Are you ready for it? Every time I have chosen a leader for my team that was like me, it has paid great dividends. Every time I have gone off the grid and taken a chance on someone in whom I saw great potential but was not like me, I have been disappointed.

When I say "like me," I'm referring to my spirit. I may not be the greatest leader in the universe, but there is one thing I know I have, and that is a good human spirit and positive attitude. I learned a long time ago that my attitude is a choice that I make in every situation. Although many have tried, I will not allow anyone else to choose my attitude for me. John Maxwell taught that if Joe and Bill have a problem, and Joe and Jim have a problem, and if Joe and Sue have a problem, who has the problem? Joe does, but he thinks that Bill, Jim, and Sue are the problem. Do you know anyone like that?

I want to help someone right now. If you are like me, when you have a problem with someone, your default reaction is typically to examine yourself and figure out what you've done that has disturbed this person so profoundly. I was praying about this some time ago and here's what God said to me: "Are you walking with me? Are you daily letting me speak to you from my word? Are you praying and daily seeking me? Are you under spiritual authority? Do you have integrity with your wife and children?" I answered yes to every one of those questions. The conclusion then was obvious: I was not the problem. I hope your answers to those same questions will give you as much peace as they gave me.

And while I'm talking about surrounding myself with people who have my attitude, let me add one more observation. Every pastor reading this has had people transfer into his/her church from another congregation, either from across town or from around the country. What most transfers do not understand is that one church is not just like another church. The reason for this is that no two pastors are alike. I am not on a power trip when I say that it is incumbent upon the move-ins to adjust themselves to the new anointing they are now under.

In Numbers 11, God told Moses to take the seventy elders into the prayer meeting tent, and he would take the *spirit* (lower case indicating his human spirit) that was upon Moses and place it upon them. This is symbolic of what must happen in every transferred attender in every congregation. Church attenders who just come and go and view the pastor as a hireling will never be promoted by God. But there must be a conscious and spiritual decision to come under that man or woman of God's anointing before there can be spiritual development and growth.

When I was young, I had great reverence for my pastor. During a worship service he invited anyone who was sick to come forward for prayer. I bolted from my mother, made my way to the front, and received prayer. When I came back my mother was upset with me. Why did you go up there? She asked. "You're not sick." I said, "But Mom, I just wanted to feel my pastor's hand on my head."

She wiped a tear from her eye and said, "Never mind."

I have thought of that through the years. Even at a young age I seemed to understand that I needed to intentionally come under the covering of my spiritual authority. Notice what Psalm 133:1–2 says on this subject:

> Behold, how good and how pleasant it is for
> brethren to dwell together in unity! It is like the
> precious oil upon the head, running down on the

beard, the beard of Aaron, running down on the edge of his garments.

I know from the scripture and from experience that anointing flows downward. If you want an anointing, you cannot receive it all by yourself; you must first come under it. If people want to make your church their spiritual home, that's fine. But until they come under your spiritual authority there will not be much growth or forward movement for them. And if you attempt to promote them without that spiritual transaction, it will not go well.

Perhaps everything I have shared in this chapter could be summarized with these words by Paul: "Imitate me, just as I also imitate Christ" (1 Cor. 11:1). This Christlike leader fellowshipped Jesus Christ, as substantiated by the fruit of his life!

CHAPTER 11

×∙×∙×∙●∙✕∙✕∙✕∙●∙✕∙×∙×

CHRISTLIKE LEADERS ARE FAMOUS IN THEIR FAMILY

*These all continued with one accord in prayer
and supplication, with the women and Mary the
mother of Jesus, and with His brothers (Acts 1:14).*

"Success is having the people closest to me,
love and respect me the most."—John Maxwell

W e do not usually think of Jesus as being a family man. He
never married, and he had no natural children. I have often
wondered about the nature of Jesus's relationships with his
mother and half-siblings. I have also mused about the attitude his
family had toward him after his baptism. Was it familial, professional, or rabbi/disciple? Would it ever be the same again? Was he
condescending toward his siblings? Did he demonstrate superiority,
authority, or demand anything from them? Was it ever awkward?
Did he speak to them as he spoke to his disciples?

At the age of twelve we catch a glimpse of Jesus's future, including his anointing and brilliance in the temple while reasoning with the doctors of the law. Luke 2:52 says that after this episode, he submitted himself to his parents. When he turned thirty and launched his ministry, the dynamic with his parents and siblings shifted. His first miracle was instigated by his mother, who may have been slightly shaken when in response he appeared exasperated and called her "woman." Later when Jesus was in the vicinity, Mary rounded up her other sons and sought an audience with him. He had been busy lately and hadn't come to see her, so she may have felt she needed to make an appointment.

Right in the middle of his rebuke of the evil and adulterous generation that was seeking a sign, someone interrupted with the message that his family wanted to see him. He looked at his rapt audience and said, "Who is my mother and who are my brothers?' He gestured toward his disciples and said, "Here are my mother and my brothers—the ones who do the will of my Father in heaven." (See Matthew 12:48–50.) I'm sure this apparent rebuff did not sit too well with his family, at least not initially.

These episodes make it appear to the cursory observer that Jesus broke ties with his immediate family and started a cult. After all, he was at Lazarus's house more than his mother's house. But if this were true, Jesus's mother and siblings would have written him off as the black sheep and grieved the loss of their relationship with him. Nothing could be further from the truth. With these familial observations, the Gospel evangelist clearly demonstrated that Jesus was focused on his mission, that he now belonged to the redemption of the whole world, and was soon going to lay down his life for his friends—and his family (John 15:13).

Was Jesus famous or infamous in his family? Did his family celebrate his mission and feel partnered in his ministry, or did they resent him for sacrificing them on the altar of his ministry? This is never a good trade, but it happens all the time in the ministry. Some well-intentioned church leaders have unwittingly made this mistake because they are particularly vulnerable in this tricky area of balancing family and ministry. Our mission is an important spiritual calling, but we create unnecessary tension when we become focused on our goals and intolerant of interruptions. Then conflict and frustration results when we don't understand why our family can't figure this out.

We must not miss what scripture tells us about Jesus's integrity with his family and his ministry, even though perhaps we must read somewhat between the lines. The opening verse of this chapter reveals that Jesus never lost integrity with his family:

> *These all continued with one accord in prayer*
> *and supplication, with the women and Mary the*
> *mother of Jesus, and with His brothers (Acts 1:14).*

It would not fit Jesus's profile to argue that because he was now functioning as Messiah that he completely disconnected from his family.

We assume that Joseph had died prior to the launching of Jesus's ministry because scripture is silent about him after the episode when Jesus was twelve. We know that his brothers struggled to figure out what to do with Jesus. Matthew 13:57 says they were offended by him, and John 7:5 says they did not believe in him. And yet they could not discount thirty years of his life of integrity among them and their overall family wellness. Jesus made a special postresurrection appearance just for James (1 Cor. 15:7). Author Herbert Lockyer observed it was after this appearance that "we find the 'brethren of the Lord' joined with the apostles and the women together in the upper chamber" (Acts 1:14).[15]

Perhaps the greatest gesture of the respect Jesus's family had for him was when they showed up for the crowning moment of his ministry in the upper room on the Day of Pentecost. A few days before this initial outpouring of the Spirit, Jesus's resurrection was witnessed by more than five hundred people, but now only 120 had assembled to receive the promise of the Father. Mary and her other sons were

---

[15] Herbert Lockyer, *All the Men of the Bible* (Grand Rapids, MI: Zondervan, 1958), 171.

among those who were filled during that initial outpouring of the Holy Spirit. In fact, Peter declared Jesus to be the baptizer of the Holy Spirit: "This Jesus God has raised up, of which we are all witnesses. Therefore, being exalted to the right hand of God, and having received from the Father the promise of the Holy Spirit, He poured out this which you now see and hear" (Acts 2:32–33).

It would be difficult if not impossible to imagine how amazed Jesus's half-brothers and sisters were, having grown up with him and knowing every nuance of his life, only to discover their big brother was the Savior of the world. Now they needed to believe he was the Son of God, that redemption was in his blood, and salvation was in his name. I smile when I think about Jesus's family receiving water baptism on the Day of Pentecost in his name (Acts 2:38–41). What does this say about Jesus's integrity with his family? Now they were twice family, naturally and spiritually his brothers and sisters.

Perhaps after they were filled with the Holy Spirit, Mary and Jesus's brothers finally saw the bigger picture of why Jesus behaved as he did throughout his ministry. It also should be noted that James became the pastor of the first church in Jerusalem. He was present at the conference when the apostles decided what to do about the Gentile problem. After hearing speeches from Apostles Peter, Paul, and Barnabas, it was James who then spoke up, and with authority summarized the solution to the satisfaction of the apostles, elders, and the whole church. (See Acts 15:13–21.) I'm sure his big brother was proud of him that day!

In chapter six I shared statistics revealing that most leaders in ministry see their calling as an occupational hazard for their family. I can understand this, but I do not relate to it. Too many leaders assume that because their family is under their roof that they're also on their bus. This is a natural but dangerous assumption. Family health is sort of like one's breath: never assume it's good. Something is wrong if a church leader is loved and trusted by ministry but loathed and mistrusted by his family.

Paul provided the resume of a church leader in 1 Timothy 3:2–5:

> A bishop then must be blameless, the husband of one wife, temperate, sober-minded, of good behavior, hospitable, able to teach; not given to wine, not violent, not greedy for money, but gentle, not quarrelsome, not covetous; one who rules his own house well, having his children in submission with all reverence (for if a man does not know how to rule his own house, how will he take care of the church of God?).

Church leaders earn the right to lead God's people, not by earning a degree or by being elected to an office, but by leading themselves well first, and then their family. I had the advantage of growing up in the home of a called man of God who qualified to lead God's people because of how he led himself, his wife, and children. My father, Wendell C. Gleason, was never a pastor, but he was an ordained minister who spent the best thirty-five years of his life training young people for ministry.

Our local church shared a campus with a small Bible college. After my dad's discharge from the Army Air Force in 1946, he and my mom moved to St. Paul, where he matriculated as a student to train for ministry. The college president recognized his maturity and gifting, and invited him to join the faculty before the end of his freshman year. My siblings and I were born over the next eleven years.

For twenty-one years, Dad traveled the months of June and July with chorales and quartets, recruiting students. He worked five days a week from 8:00 a.m. to 6:00 p.m., and from 8:00 a.m. to 2:00 p.m. on Saturday. On Sunday, our family spent most of the day in church for morning and evening services. Although it was upsetting for me as a youngster to watch my dad pull out of the driveway every June, knowing I would not see him for a long time, I never felt as though he preferred his job/ministry over me or our family. I knew when he came back home, we were going on a two- or three-week vacation somewhere fun, and I would have him all to myself. What ministry took away from his family, he always found a way to give back. He maintained healthy relationships with Mom and us four kids. He kept all of his accounts short and never let the sun go down on his wrath.

Sometimes when I pray, I call on the God of Abraham, Isaac, Jacob, Turner (my grandfather), and Wendell. My grandchildren Melina, Cohen, Marigold, and Rosemary can add, "Stan, and their parents (Justin and Ana or Daniel and Marissa)" to their preamble. I believe that families have spirits, and if there is such a thing as generational curses then there must also be generational blessings! If our family is known for anything, it would have to be peace and harmony, both literally and figuratively. My dad and siblings and I produced three vocal projects and participated in numerous others. We all love God, each other, and cherish time together.

When my youngest son Caleb was fifteen, I was invited to give a devotion to the Denver Broncos when they came to town to face the Kansas City Chiefs (the 2020 NFL World Champions). We had baptized one of their rookie players (Chris Harris Jr.), who then married a young lady from our congregation. After his baptism, I shared with Chris that I felt like one day God would give me a voice in professional athletes' lives. He must have put in a good word for me because a few days later I was contacted by their director of player development, Jerry Butler, who extended the invitation.

Jerry named the hotel where they were staying and suggested a time to meet him in the lobby. He said I could bring two guests, so I chose my sons Justin and Caleb. He also laid out the rules: no photos, no autographs, no talking about my favorite NFL football team (the heartbreaking Minnesota Vikings), and no yelling. (I wondered what guest's idiotic actions had caused them to formulate *that* rule.) They said no one would introduce me, and my job was to stand up, speak up for twenty minutes, and then shut up.

Promptly at 7:30 p.m., I stood up, turned around to face about half of the team (devotions were voluntary). I quickly perused my audience but was disappointed that Peyton Manning was not in the room. I took a deep breath, opened my mouth, and was about to begin when the door opened and Peyton walked in. He came straight up to me, introduced himself (as if I didn't know who he was), thanked me for coming, and took his seat in the second row.

My subject was "What Is Success in Life?" I explained that I had adopted John Maxwell's definition of success: success in life is having the people closest to me love and respect me the most. To illustrate this point, I had Caleb come and stand beside me. He's tall, red-headed, humble, and easily embarrassed. I'm sure he was intimidated to be standing in front of those multimillion-dollar athletes.

I shared with the Broncos that I was an elected official of a religious organization comprised of forty thousand congregations around the world. When I walk into our general boardroom, there are one hundred chairs on the floor and four chairs at the head table. I sit in one of those four chairs. I admitted that I would like to have the respect of those men at that table and in that room. But more than that, I wanted the respect of the young man standing next to me. I admitted that I could fool those men in that room, but I could not fool the young man who eats Cheerios at my table every morning. If he loves and respects me, then I am successful. I felt like this message would resonate with men who have had the world at their feet their entire lives, and who perhaps struggle with developing authentic relationships.

As Caleb began to walk back to his seat, Peyton Manning clapped his hands loudly and shouted, "All right, Caleb!" Caleb ducked his head, turned beet red, and it cracked everybody up when they saw how embarrassed he was. After my talk was over, Peyton walked all the way across the room, sought out Caleb, shook his hand, and sincerely thanking him for coming. He didn't have to do that, but he knew he would make a teenage boy's day and give him an unforgettable moment. Incidentally, five years later when Caleb introduced me to speak during a chapel service at his Christian college, I responded that I had just been introduced by a young man who was once been applauded by Peyton Manning.

I have been in full-time ministry for forty-two years. All but seven of those years I have served in some official capacity beyond my local ministry assignment. When I was unexpectedly elected as a district superintendent serving 165 congregations, I gave an impromptu acceptance speech. I told them that my priorities were God, my wife Marlene, my children, the congregation I serve, and then those who had just elected me. I humbly informed them that if they were all right with being fifth on my list that we would get along just fine. If not, they might want to elect someone else next term. It must have worked because they were gracious enough to elect me four more times before I was chosen by the voters of our organization to serve as a national leader. My greatest calling and election, however, is to serve God, my wife, and my children.

When my oldest son Justin was fifteen, we were having an escalated discussion. I don't remember what the issue was, but I'm sure it had something to do with him attempting to discover his independence against my better judgment. We both knew I had a church-related responsibility that night, and it was almost time for me to leave. I sternly informed him that we would finish our little chat when I came back home. As I was backing the car out of the driveway, I felt a check; it literally seemed like the Lord called me a "jerk." Then the gentle voice of God seemed to say to me, "You think you're leaving your son to go do your most important work, but you're actually driving away from your most important work."

I rolled my eyes, hit the brakes, put the car in drive, and pulled back into the garage. I called someone to take my place that night, then knocked on Justin's bedroom door. When he opened the door, he was surprised to see me standing there. I explained to him that he was more important to me than the church or anything else in the world. We quickly brought our disagreement to a redemptive conclusion. Fifteen or so years later, when Justin (our elected associate pastor) was preaching to our congregation, he recalled that story. I was amazed at the great and lasting impression a small gesture of familial integrity had made on him.

Christlike church leaders will have integrity with their family. I've always felt that the health and wellness of a church leader's immediate family is the most important box to check on their resume. If I had ten thousand worshippers on our campus this Sunday but one of my children was not in relationship with Jesus Christ, I would have a great emptiness in my heart. Conversely, there is no greater joy than to have my children imitate my model and embrace my faith.

We all understand that when children become adults, they will choose their path. There are very few, if any, scenarios more painful for a pastor than a child departing the faith. It is impossible to not take it personally, no matter how careful the parents have been. It's tough enough for children who grow up in the parsonage without their dad prioritizing pastoring over parenting. Additionally, church people can place unrealistic expectations on the pastor's children and expect them to be perfect. The only thing worse is when the pastor demands his children be examples for the other kids in the church.

One of my colleagues shared with me that his wife fell on the floor and agonized for three days after their son announced his girlfriend was pregnant, and that he was charting another course than following theirs. I recognize the fact that Satan attacks and distracts pastors through their families. But I refuse to accept that my calling is an occupational hazard for my family. Why would God call anyone into the ministry at the expense of losing their family if this was his expectation?

I know there are some church leaders' children who are offended at the church for how the congregation treated their parents or for taking their parents away from them, but I think most tragedies occur when the leaders' children feel like their parents have placed them in the back seat of their priorities. We all understand there are times when the ministry takes away from the family, but whenever this happened to me, I tried to keep score. What I mean is, if the ministry took something away from the family, I found a way to give it back. For example, if someone in the congregation gave us a gift card to a restaurant, I made sure my children knew who gave it to us while we were in the moment enjoying a meal together. If someone baked a pie or gave us a turkey, I gave credit to the givers because I wanted my children to feel blessed and not denied. Consequently, my children's heroes and best friends are in the church.

Some of the greatest church leaders I've ever known suffered at least one spiritual casualty in their immediate family. I have known a few church leaders who were unsuccessful in making disciples out of any of their children. One could be a mistake, but two might be a pattern. Neither of Samuel's sons, Joel and Abijah, followed in his steps. First Samuel 8:3 says, "But his sons did not walk in his ways; they turned aside after dishonest gain, took bribes, and perverted justice."

Samuel obviously did not have the respect of his sons. He is never described in scripture as they are, so where did they develop this unacceptable behavior? Could Samuel have been so busy with his ministry that he lost relationship with his sons? Their rejection by the nation of Israel must have crushed him. God explained that Israel had rejected him and not Samuel, but had Samuel done a better job of reaching for fame in his family, it may have been a different story.

How could Samuel know the reputation of his sons and yet attempt to appoint them as judges over Israel? This alone is problematic and perhaps exposes a parental blind spot. I lay this responsibility at the feet of Samuel. I know he was out and about doing the important business of anointing other men's sons as kings for Israel, but there was no anointing on his own sons. Some have said that I have built a reputation for making room for the next generation of church leaders, but woe unto me if I did that for other men's sons but not my own.

There are reasons for everything. No parent wins the "my kids are saved, sanctified, and called to the ministry" lottery. It takes a lot of work, prayer, agonizing, and anxious moments. Only God can choose to call them, and no parent should make the mistake of trying to do this in God's stead. It is the greatest feeling in the world to see your own children begin to connect with God and become saved by his grace. It is an added blessing if God chooses to place his calling upon them.

Parents are instructed to train up their children in the way they should go, so when they are older they will not depart from that way (Prov. 22:6). The proverbs are not promises; rather, they are wise and generally true statements. If we act in a certain way, then the results are usually predictable. This verse literally means that parents can instill the right choice in their children. Not every pastor's child is called into the ministry, but they are likely targets. If I were God and looking for choice vessels to call into the ministry, this is where I would look first. Think about it: these kids have been receiving on-the-job training their entire lives.

In contrast to Samuel, another man of God named Philip was blessed to have at least four children who were called into the ministry. Acts 21:8–9 informs us that he had four daughters who were morally pure and they each possessed the gift of prophecy. This is unusual, and I have never known the equal. Philip must have felt so blessed to have four children living virtuous lives, and on top of that, they were walking with the God who had saved, called, and gifted them. How did this happen? Not by accident, I can assure you.

Philip had been planting the seeds of family success for a long time. He was chosen by the church and then ordained by the apostles to serve tables in the daily administration of the first church in Jerusalem (Acts 6). His résumé, along with the others chosen, included having a good reputation, being full of the Holy Spirit and full of wisdom. Philip was respected and highly esteemed by those around him. When you read the phrase "full of" in the New Testament, it means "to be controlled by." What a joy and privilege for these girls to be raised in the home of a man whose spirit was being controlled by the Holy Spirit and wisdom.

Not only did the community respect Philip, but his daughters certainly did too. Had they not respected him and had he not had credibility with them, they would not have given themselves to the Lord as they did. Philip was destined for more than just waiting on tables, however. He was under the spiritual authority of the apostles, and apparently had a call on his life to preach the word. The apostles sent him to Samaria, fulfilling Jesus's prophecy of Acts 1:8. Philip preached Jesus, and this message was followed by miracles; demons were cast out, believers were baptized, and the city was filled with joy. This is the fruit of a church leader with godly credibility.

Philip had eventually settled in Caesarea by the time Paul came through on a missionary journey. There are many places Paul could have stayed, but he chose Philip's house. When you read Acts 21:8–11 you can understand why. Paul was a man who was led by the Spirit, and he knew that the atmosphere of Philip's house would be spiritual. His daughters were continually ministering to the Lord and prophesying, and the prophet Agabus came to visit as well. Philip was not only famous in Samaria and throughout the churches in Caesarea, but more significantly, he was famous in his family.

Marlene and I have been married forty-three years and have been blessed with four godly children and now four young grandchildren. Dr. James Dobson once said that you won't know if you have successfully transferred your values to your children until you see your grandchildren, so we shall see. By the time a man realizes his dad was right, he usually has a son who thinks he's wrong.

Our two oldest children are married, and the two youngest are yet at home. Our youngest was born the day after I turned forty-one. Some smart aleck asked what I was thinking to have children in my old age. I responded snarkily, "Well, Marlene and I wanted to have grandchildren, but we didn't want to wait, so we had our own, so cry me a river, build a bridge, and get over it."

I'm sure that our home is not perfect, but by the grace of God, our four adult children are walking with God and are committed to ministry and the mission to go make disciples. Our oldest son Justin was called to the ministry when I took him with me to a youth camp in Wisconsin where I was invited to preach. One night after the service I couldn't find Justin. I searched the food area, the basketball and volleyball courts, and playground. Last, I walked over to the tabernacle that was now dark—the service had been over for an hour.

When I opened the door, I heard some muffled praying and crying out to God. After stumbling around in the dark, I finally found him wedged between the back wall and stage. When he crawled out, his face was red and his eyes and cheeks were wet with tears. I said, "Justin, what happened to you tonight?"

He said, "Dad, I've got this fire burning inside of me."

I said, "What do you think it means?"

He replied, "I believe that God has called me to preach." After graduating from high school, he completed a four-year Bible college program. He came home to be our student pastor, but several years ago was elected as our associate pastor.

Our oldest daughter Marissa was my secretary for four years after finishing two years of Bible college. She later earned a bachelor's degree in leadership. She came to me one day and said, "Dad, do I have to marry a preacher?"

I responded with "Now why would you ask me a question like that? I've never put any pressure on you to marry a preacher."

She said, "Well, our whole family is filled with preachers, and I thought it's what you wanted."

I said, "Listen, I don't even care if your husband is saved, provided he treats you like a queen, works hard, and doesn't ask me for money."

She knew I was joking about the "not being saved" comment but not about the money part.

She married Daniel, who was a registered nurse at a children's hospital in Milwaukee. After about three years of marriage, Daniel shared with me that God had been dealing with him about answering a calling on his life. He asked me what I thought about him applying for his ministerial license. I chuckled and asked him if he had talked to Marissa about it. Suffice it to say, she married a preacher anyway, so rack up another preacher for the family.

Micaela has demonstrated a great heart for God since she was very young. She earned a bachelor's degree in education and is now a public schoolteacher. She has a passion to connect with people of other cultures here at home, but has also taken many missions trips abroad. She also serves as director of junior high ministry at our church. Her little brother Caleb was called to preach at a children's church camp at the age of eight. He has just returned home from four years at a Christian college, earning his bachelor's degree in Christian Ministry. He serves as our student discipleship pastor and has begun a master's program in theological studies. He has a heart to make disciples.

I cannot fully express what it means to my wife and me to be partnered in ministry with our children. Any one of them at any time could have chosen a path other than the one we led, but we are thrilled beyond words that they love God in word and deed. I give God and my wife all the glory for our blessed reality. I cannot thank

God enough for her heart for him and the common-sense integrity with which she conducts her life. I've always believed the woman of the house sets the atmosphere of the home. If you have that in your house, you are destined to become famous in your family.

Many years ago, I was teaching a Bible study in a home where the man of the house had been an alcoholic for many years. His wife and two young children would sit attentively at the kitchen table as I taught the word of God, but the husband sat around the corner in the living room with the TV blaring.

Early one evening when I knocked on the door, their little boy answered. When he saw me, his eyes got big and he whirled around and shouted, "Hey, Mom, God's here!" I chuckled at first but thought about it later and realized he was exactly right. I'd like to think that I was bringing God to their home as well as to our home every time I cross the threshold. (Incidentally, both husband and wife in that home were eventually born again and are faithful to this day.)

Noah and Lot each brought amazing God assignments to their families, but notice their much different responses. Noah announced to his family that God had told him he was going to destroy the earth with water and he should build an ocean-going vessel that, in today's equivalent, was longer than a football field. He knew he was famous in his family the moment his wife, sons, and daughters-in-law did not doubt or question him. They esteemed him as a man who found grace in the eyes of the Lord. Lot, on the other hand, couldn't seem to get his family to believe his equally remarkable warning from God. His sons-in-law thought he was joking, his wife looked back and was turned into a pillar of salt, and later his daughters got him drunk and seduced him. Was it their family culture and personal walk with God that made the difference?

My grandfather, Turner Hubbell Gleason, is famous in our family but not because he was a Vaudeville performer, actor, and singer before he was saved by the Grace of God. He isn't famous among us because, while in art school in Minneapolis before the turn of the twentieth century, he painted a charcoal sketch of Chief Ogallala Fire who fought at Little Big Horn. He isn't famous because he traveled with a national itinerant tent revival evangelist and opened the services in concert with his melodic yet booming baritone voice. He isn't famous because he operated the elevator in Oregon City, Oregon, that connected the upper city with the lower city and he knew virtually everyone in town. He isn't famous because an Oregon City street was named after him. He isn't famous because he died from a brain hemorrhage at the age of ninety-three without having a sick day in his life.

But he is famous in his family because during the Great Depression he received a certified letter informing him that he was the benefactor of a 4.3-million-dollar estate. The catch was he would have to move to England to collect the payout as prescribed by law. This was a no-brainer decision, but not in the way you might think. He was raising eight children in a house whose backyard joined the backyard of their church. The entire family was very involved in their congregation. He was the pastor's friend (also his brother-in-law), he led the worship service, his wife was the pianist, and the children all played instruments in the orchestra. It was a good church and his kids were all headed in the right direction.

He tried to determine if there was a suitable congregation in London where he could replace what he had at home. Discovery was difficult, so finding none, he wrote a letter back to the law firm releasing them to pass the inheritance down to the next one in line. Some would have called him a fool, but this is what made him famous in his family. His legacy now includes over 150 direct descendants: twenty-three credentialed ministers, two Bible college presidents, missionaries, evangelists, pastors, organizational leaders, overcoming Christians now to the sixth generation.

Family fame is attainable, and is not that difficult if you build lifetime relationships with Jesus Christ and those closest to you.

CHAPTER 12

CHRISTLIKE LEADERS HAVE THE CHRISTLIKE TOUCH

I am the vine, you are the branches. He who abides in Me, and I in him, bears much fruit; for without Me you can do nothing. If anyone does not abide in Me, he is cast out as a branch and is withered; and they gather them and throw them into the fire, and they are burned. If you abide in Me, and My words abide in you, you will ask what you desire, and it shall be done for you. By this My Father is glorified, that you bear much fruit; so you will be My disciples (John 15:5–9).

"It's always nice when preachers are Christians."—J. T. Pugh

Jesus did all things well. In turn, he informed us how to do all things well. Therefore, the goal of church leaders should be to study Jesus, learn of Jesus, and to accurately imitate him. Our leadership model should closely resemble Jesus in our manner and presentation. I am not referring to staff structure or administrative style; rather, I'm referring to becoming like his person.

Is it possible to become like him? John apparently affirmed it was when he wrote, "Love has been perfected among us in this: that we may have boldness in the day of judgment; because as He is, so are we in this world" (1 John 4:17). Paul apparently agreed as well when he wrote in Ephesians 4:13, "Till we all come to the unity of the faith and of the knowledge of the Son of God, to a perfect man, to the measure of the stature of the fullness of Christ." Paul was indicating that the manner and attitude of Jesus is still the measure of spiritual maturity in every believer, but especially so for those in leadership. The goal of church leadership is to model Jesus. If how we act, what we say, or how we treat others is not like him, then we are stunted. We do not measure up to the stature of the fullness of Christ and therefore are not accurately representing him in this world.

Nobody likes to be misquoted. Perhaps all of us have had our words taken out of context and used to misrepresent us. There is little more in life that is more painful than to have our words, actions, or motives misjudged by someone who did not give our full representation to others. As a pastor, I cannot have someone on my staff or anyone close to me who does not represent my attitude, actions, and values to others. There are few things in life that upset me more than someone in my inner circle going rogue and failing to represent me well. I'm sure you feel the same way, and so does Jesus.

I am quite certain that Jesus Christ is disappointed, if not grieved, when he is ill-represented by church leadership. We all have witnessed very poor presentations of Jesus Christ. I am not speaking about theology, but about biography. Someone can have impeccable biblical theology but be far from Christ's biography. Theology means nothing and is useless unless it becomes biography. John wrote, "In the beginning was the Word." That is theology. Then he presented Jesus to us: "And the Word become flesh and dwelt among us." Now that is biography!

In John 15, Jesus commanded us to abide in him so we could be extensions of him. In Jesus's metaphor, the vine is an extension of the branch. Who could say where the branch ends and the vine begins? He could have said, "You be oranges and I'll be the apple," but he didn't. The branch and vine are of the same substance, one supplying the other with a constant flow of resources and influence so as to accurately represent the DNA and purpose of the branch. He challenged us to keep our lives attached to his in every way and stressed that without this vital connection we can do nothing. If we are vines growing out from his branch, then it should be difficult for others to discern where he ends and we begin.

Jesus's declaration that without him we can do nothing means we cannot accomplish any eternal purpose through a strictly human attempt. However, is there an underlying message? Could he be intimating that when we are without him and without his power at work in us, then what we are doing is *not him*...which means we are doing nothing.

Paul said in Romans 8:9, "Now if anyone does not have the Spirit of Christ, he is not His." What does the phrase "the Spirit of Christ" mean? Of course, we understand this statement to refer to the infilling of the Holy Spirit, but being filled with the Spirit does not guarantee the immediate manifestation of the Spirit of the man Christ Jesus. Being filled and being controlled by the Spirit are not the same thing. I know Spirit-filled believers who do not represent Jesus Christ well in attitude, how they treat others, or how they live their personal lives. Paul said in Romans 8:14, "For as many as are led by the Spirit of God, these are sons of God." How tragic it would be for a church leader or any believer to have been filled with the Spirit, but not "have the Spirit of Christ"!

According to Paul, those who cry "Abba, Father" (Rom. 8:15) receive the Spirit of adoption. But apparently, not everyone who receives adoption by the Spirit is also being *led* by the Spirit! Being led by the Spirit of Jesus Christ should be the byproduct of being filled with the Spirit. We should seek to be led by the Spirit of Christ in every kingdom endeavor, great or small.

What do our lives look like when we are led by the Spirit of Jesus Christ? Everything Jesus touched or spoke to instantly improved. At the touch of his hand or the sound of his life-giving words or the moment he made a decision, people were healed, delivered, improved, uplifted, increased, or taken to a new level. What impact does your touch have? What happens to the atmosphere in the room when you walk in or when you open your mouth? Do your decisions tend to turn things right-side up or upside down? If the wellness of Jesus is your model, your influence will always make a positive impact. If not, you may be led by something, but it's not the Spirit of Christ.

Every building Jesus entered manifested a positive change in the atmosphere by the time he exited, including the Temple (cleansing), the synagogue (frequent healings), Zacchaeus's house (salvation and restitution), Peter's house (his mother-in-law healed), Jairus's house (his daughter raised from the dead), or even his own tomb (still empty). Every time he was in or near a boat where the disciples were present, conditions improved quickly (storm stilled, walking on the boisterous waves, nets breaking with a record catch of fish). Every time an item was placed in his hands, something special happened: mud balls became eyeballs, one small lunch fed a multitude, previously ignored children were welcomed and blessed, lepers were cleansed, driven nails opened fountains of redemption. Every time Jesus spoke to hurting people, healing and revelation followed: "Go and sin no more," "Go show yourselves to the priest," "Give me to drink," "Behold my hands and my side," "Father, forgive them."

John Maxwell's philosophy is that everything rises and falls with leadership. If the leaders are doing a good job, then everything they touch, speak to, or approach is going to rise to a new level. I know leaders who have placed their hands on nothing and turned it into something. I also have known leaders (in title only) who were given something and turned it into nothing. I have known pastors who whittled their congregation down to half. In one extreme case, a pastor successfully emptied the church, sold the property, pocketed the cash, and left town.

I lack any significant mechanical or construction skills; consequently, my wife's toolbox is in much better condition than mine. I inherited my mechanical ineptness from my dad. He had to pay for everything to be fixed or built, and so do I. His mother used to tease him and say, "Wendell, put down that wheelbarrow. You know you're not mechanical." I have always been intimidated by construction projects or other hands-on jobs. Early in my pastoral career my plan was to take on discouraged congregations with room to grow in the sanctuary, fill it up, and move on. (This was before the advent of multiple church services.) By the grace of God, we accomplished this twice. The only problem was that after the second time we were never quite ready to move on.

We have been serving that second congregation for thirty-three years. Our attendance has doubled two and one-half times. The last sixteen of those years we have enjoyed our new eighty-three-acre campus and forty-one-thousand-square-foot worship/educational facility. We are currently in a multimillion-dollar, thirty-six-month capital stewardship campaign to expand the children's ministry, enlarge the sanctuary, and finish the event center. We have not broken any records, but we are thankful and excited to see this congregation flourish and enlarge their footprint in the community.

Speaking of the Christlike touch, one interesting feature of our ministry emerged as a pattern. I have prayed over many couples (around ten) who had been married for over ten years without producing children. All but one couple are parents now. One couple asked for prayer, so I told them when the time was right, I would call for them. On Father's Day (the third Sunday of June) I felt impressed to pray over them. Their son was born at the end of the following March. Do the math. After the excited father shared this miracle with the congregation, some men would see me coming and began to run in the opposite direction—especially the father who has nine children.

Soon after we came to Kansas City, God made it very clear to me what our assignment was. In the first eighteen months of our pastorate, fourteen families moved in from out of town and started attending our church. At first it felt like we had won the move-in lottery. At that time, we were a small congregation, so fourteen families made a significant impact. I don't ask new families a lot of questions, but as they became more oriented, they began to share their stories. Every story had a common thread: they had all suffered in some measure at the hands of unhealthy church leadership.

It wasn't long until the Lord made it clear to me that our assignment was to be a healing center where he could send good people who were about to give up. He would trust us with the discouraged and disillusioned to be spiritually healed, and to restore their confidence in church leadership. I felt a strong conviction that if I failed to provide a healthy, healing atmosphere that souls would be lost. Our congregation was a perfect setting for this special work of the Holy Spirit: I was a pastor who had been beaten up by a church; they were a church that had been beaten down by leadership. We understood each other perfectly. We started lavishing love on people. In fact, after we had been serving them about six months, one long-time church member told me I was like a Band-Aid for their wounds.

There is nothing unique about our story; every pastor and every congregation is called to do the same. It's just that some understand it and do it well. In a culture of Christlike wellness, they become purveyors of peace; others who are unwell themselves become purveyors of pain. I learned a long time ago that hurting people hurt people. How many sick patients have entered medical centers only to contract a worse condition than the one for which they sought relief? Jesus condemned the Pharisees because they traveled the world over to make disciples who, under their care, became twofold children of hell. These misguided converts thought they were being saved, but because their doctors of the law were themselves infected, they could not find healing. One of Nordstrom's slogans is: "The only difference in stores is the way they treat their customers." This also could apply to congregations.

Too many pastors and church leaders have become jaded over time due to chronic attacks by the dysfunctional people they are attempting to serve. Church leaders worth their salt have been criticized at least once, but like a Timex watch, they take a licking and keep on ticking. I don't know where my critics are today, but I know where I am. I stand humble and healthy and well, and that by the grace of God. The people I have the privilege of touching are improving, healing, and gaining ground every day.

In John 15, Jesus made it clear that he is the fruit inspector. When he examines the branch of our life, he is looking for one thing: fruit. For too long church leaders have placed the expectation of faithfulness and not fruitfulness on their followers. Most pastors are happy if their members come to church twice a week, pay their tithes, sing in the choir, and don't cause trouble. That may show faithfulness but not necessarily fruitfulness. Someone can be faithful without being fruitful, but the presence of fruit always demonstrates faithfulness. Although this book is not about unfruitful church members, I covered the subject in my previous book, *Follow to Lead: The Journey of a Disciple Maker*.

If anyone reading this happens to stumble upon the perfect church, don't join it. You might ruin everything. Despite the universally known reality that there is no such thing as a perfect church, well-intentioned pastors seem to make it their goal to create one. They become part-time psychiatrists, police officers, drill sergeants, or world federation wrestlers in a futile attempt to either psychoanalyze, arrest, scream at, or body slam their members in hopes of inducing utopian behavior. The more scrutiny and control one-man exercises over a congregation the more dysfunctional and cultlike it will become. Helicopter pastors who hover over their members produce immature believers who lack personal spiritual convictions, who can't make a godly decision by themselves, and who run to "papa" pastor for their every need and decision.

I heard a joke about a man who had to ditch his small plane in the sea due to mechanical failure. He swam safely to a one-acre tropical island. Ten years later a passing boat noticed him frantically waving his arms and shouting. He jumped into the sea and swam out to the boat. They joyfully welcomed him aboard, and as the captain was backing the boat away from the shore, he noticed three small huts just beyond the beach line. Curious, he asked the man if he had built all three huts, and if so, what had he used them for. The grateful man replied, "Yes, I built them. The middle hut is where I lived. The hut on the right is where I went to church. The hut on the left is where I used to go to church."

Dysfunction can be found within any institution or anywhere there is more than one person. Local churches are susceptible to dysfunction because authority is needed but not always qualified.

Insecurity in leaders will not allow them to trust people or God to do the right thing. They feel compelled to control and micromanage their loyal subjects. They interpret any misstep as a direct attack against their authority and a threat to their success of perfecting you. For instance, one young man in our congregation told me his former pastor's wife made him bring his pay stubs to church and prove his tithing was commensurate with his income. And on that note, I have found that church leaders who overreach and are hard on people in certain areas can inadvertently be revealing their own struggles. Insecure church leaders also may find themselves dictating arbitrary rules against things they don't like or aren't good at just to show they have control over someone.

I'm the last person to try to control anyone, but as a young pastor I attempted to shoulder everyone's problems. If someone came to me for advice or counseling, I would listen, take it to heart, pray, fast, and get back to them in a few days with what I felt God had given me for them. During my first week as a fledgling pastor, a man about fifteen years my senior came to me for advice. Because I had little experience, I was reluctant to weigh in on what I thought he needed to do, so I told him I would fast and pray and get back with him soon. After a few days, I felt like God gave me direction for him and was anxious to share it. We scheduled an appointment, and I sat down with him and rattled off what I thought was the will of God for his dilemma.

Do you think he did what I advised him to do? No, and I was devastated. I had spent all that time, emotion, prayer, thought, missed meals, and suffering from new-pastor anxiety in trying to help him along his journey, and then he proceeded to do what he had already made up his mind to do before he came to see me. I realized then that most people have already decided what they want to do before they come to their pastor, so what they really want is their pastor's blessing, not their advice. Consequently, I have learned to ask just enough questions to figure out what direction they want to go, push them in that direction (if it's not contrary to the word of God), then I go have lunch. It's a perfect system.

Of course, intuitive readers know those last two sentences were tongue-in-cheek. I'm simply saying that the longer I live, my list of what I'm willing to die for is getting pared down. It breaks my heart to see people make a mess out of their lives. Life is tough enough without continually shooting oneself in the foot. On the other hand, codependent-type leaders can fret over their people's decisions to the point of exhaustion.

Years ago, I heard John Maxwell speak on the subject "I Don't Have to Survive." He said Paul had this attitude throughout his ministry. It came through when he wrote things like, "To be absent from the body is to be present with the Lord." Nobody could devastate him because he didn't have to survive the outcome of the confrontation. Every time he was challenged, he reminded himself that he already had been crucified with Christ. He just shrugged his shoulders and continued doing the will of God.

When Demas forsook him, Paul kept planting churches. When Alexander the coppersmith did him much harm, he continued preaching Jesus. When he was beaten for preaching the gospel in Philippi, he baptized the jailer. What did he get for healing a lame man in Lystra? Persecution—he was stoned, dragged out of the city, and left for dead. According to today's custom, he would have filed a lawsuit, but instead the disciples gathered around him, lifted him up, and helped him on his way to Derbe, where he proceeded to make more disciples. When he suffered shipwreck, he swam ashore and helped start a fire to warm the survivors. A venomous serpent sprang out and sank its fangs into his arm, but Paul calmly shook it off and went on to evangelize that little island. When his life was threatened by Caesar, Paul said, "Go ahead…take my head off, for to me to live is Christ, to die is gain."

What can you do with that? Nothing! You can't threaten a man who has already died. Instead of dying a thousand deaths over every crisis, catastrophe, and problem, we can embrace the theology of Paul who died once unto Christ on the road to Damascus. Perhaps we would live better if we would stop dying for other people's confusion, pain, and brokenness. We shouldn't be like the man whose cat needed its tail amputated. Not wanting to hurt the cat too badly, he cut its tail off one inch at a time. There will always be challenges, critics, misunderstandings, and threats, but don't allow the disposition of others to determine your attitude. Your attitude is your choice. You can choose with Paul to "have the same attitude toward [others] that Christ Jesus had" (Phil. 2:5, NET).

A police officer would not be an appropriate analogy of a pastor, yet some called men of God will figuratively track people down, pull them over, read them their rights, put them in handcuffs, interrogate them, and throw them in jail. I would go so far as to suggest that some church leaders have dabbled in what I would call "spiritual witchcraft." This sounds harsh, but think about it. Witchcraft is an attempt to manipulate people into a desired behavior using any spirit other than the Holy Spirit. It doesn't require a séance to invoke witchcraft. Leaders with very strong personalities who employ anger, rage, or victimization to intimidate, shame, humiliate, or put people on guilt trips have participated in it.

I have heard of leaders who required church members caught in sin to confess before the church. Where did Jesus prescribe this? I know of one pastor who discovered that someone had stolen money from a woman's purse when she had left it unattended on the pew for a few moments. The next service the pastor got up and instructed the church to march single file before the pulpit, and he demanded the guilty party to kneel there and confess the sin. Of course, nobody did. What leader in his right mind would require such humiliation? There is a biblical prescription for humility, but there is no mandate from Christ for the humiliation of others. Making an example out of church members smacks of gang, cult, or concentration camp tactics.

There can be no question that church business is messy. Paul said that Christ would present to himself a glorious church without spot, wrinkle, or blemish (Eph. 5:27). I cannot say that I have seen a church as glorious as that. But I'm not Christ. I didn't suffer, bleed, and die for the church. If he wants to call his church glorious, that is his business, but when I look at her I can see spots, wrinkles, and blemishes. So we can deduce that in Ephesians 5:27 Paul was speaking theologically, not pragmatically. Paul was painfully aware of the underbelly of the church. He once shared that he had suffered at the hand of false brethren, among numerous other tragedies (2 Cor. 11:26).

I know we can admire the perfect church, but can we love the real church? In 1979, I was a young evangelist fresh out of Bible college and newly married. Marlene and I traveled around the country with my Fender Precision Bass guitar and Baseman amplifier stowed in the back seat. We regaled congregations nightly with our humble duets and two-piece band (Marlene played the piano).

I don't know what I was thinking to drag my new bride around, in and out of other people's homes, not to mention the dreaded but inexpensive Motel 6 on our days off. One week we stayed in a Sunday school room that was separated from a one-room Christian school by a thin divider. Every morning at 8:00 a.m. sharp we were awakened by a robust version of "This Is the Day That the Lord Has Made." We had to walk across the lawn in housecoats and slippers to take a shower at the parsonage. I could not imagine treating any of my guests the same, but we were thankful for the opportunity to minister.

During a church service in Ottawa, Illinois, the pastor leaned over to me and pointed out a couple sitting in the third row from the back on the left. He told me that was her third husband. Sitting on the row were his kids, her kids, and their kids. Then he pointed out the couple sitting on the pew behind them. That was her second husband and their kids. I was hoping the pastor was through when he cited the couple on the last row, revealing that was the woman's first husband and their kids. He explained her first two failed marriages were before Christ. After her conversion, she reached out to both previous husbands and led them and their spouses to salvation. Now they were all one in the body of Christ. The pastor was celebrating these trophies of grace. It was beautiful, but messy.

A few men from our local congregation have served time in prison. At one time, I was thankful for no divorces in our congregation, but that record has long since been broken. Men and women from rehab centers have been baptized only to relapse. Thankfully, I have been spared the tragedy of infidelities in the pastoral staff members or financial mismanagement. Looked at from a positive perspective, however, we have former inmates now living overcoming lives, recovered marriages, healed divorcees, former addicts living victoriously, recovered alcoholics, and just about every category of transgression Paul addressed in 1 Corinthians 6:9–11. Take note that Paul was quick to add, "But such were some of you."

It must have broken Paul's heart to pen the words, "Demas has forsaken me…" That was dramatic enough. But then he painfully added "…having loved this present world." One might think that is inconceivable! How could this be referencing one of Paul's personal disciples? At some point, Demas had even suffered imprisonment with Paul. What stronger bonds could be forged than this? It appears to be a foregone conclusion that Demas had turned his back on God, quit following his pastor, and left the church.

But if you continue reading 2 Timothy 4:10, Paul gave one more important piece of information: "[Demas] has departed for Thessalonica." Why is this important? It matters because we know there was a redemptive congregation there. The church in Thessalonica was remarkable because Paul established it in three weeks. (How is that for turbo church planting?) By contrast, it had taken Paul months to get a foothold in Corinth. Paul commended the Christians in Thessalonica for their "work of faith, labor of love, and patience of hope" (1 Thess. 1:3). They were imitators of Paul and an example to all the believers in Macedonia and Achaia. Paul said that everywhere he went people would comment about the faith of the believers in Thessalonica. In his second letter to them he recognized their love for one another and how they endured hardships and even persecution.

If Paul would have said, "Demas has departed for Galatia"—the church that left grace and turned to legalism—I don't think Demas would have recovered even if he had darkened their door. If he had departed for Ephesus—where they had left their first love—he may not have had a second chance. What if he had departed for Corinth? Forget it. The atmosphere churned with division, tolerated sexual sin, and abused the gifts of the Spirit. Some of them failed to discern the Lord's body, which resulted in unnecessary sickness, spiritual anemia, and untimely deaths.

But thank God Demas departed for Thessalonica where there was a healthy, balanced, redemptive, and accepting congregation abounding with love for God and for one another. Did Demas ever show up there? I don't know, but if he did, I think he would have made it. Does your church have the characteristics of the church in Thessalonica? If your leadership extends the Christlike touch, Demases who have relocated to your community will have a second chance in your church.

CHAPTER 13

CHRISTLIKE LEADERS COMMIT TO PERSONAL GROWTH

And Jesus increased in wisdom and stature, and in favor with God and men (Luke 2:52).

"Aging is inevitable, but growing is optional."—Unknown

The scripture is silent on the eighteen years between this episode of Jesus at age twelve, and his baptism. We can assume that what was said of him at this developmental stage was consistently reflected in his life until the launch of his ministry at the Jordan. As Son of God, Jesus did not need to study the word, for he was the word incarnate (John 1:1). But as son of man, Jesus was required to study at the feet of a rabbi, learn a trade at the feet of Joseph, and discover his prophetic birth and destiny at the feet of Mary.

Jesus just could not be a poor representative of the mighty God whose image he bore. His intellect must be developed, his emotions must be mature, his behavior must be impeccable, his conversations must be appropriate, and his purpose must be clear. Perhaps it could be argued that had Jesus been abandoned as a babe and raised in the wilderness by wolves, as God manifested in the flesh he still would have stepped on the stage of Galilee, Judea, and Samaria and changed the world. Thus it is pointless to argue how significant Jesus's formative years were in shaping the effectiveness of his ministry. All we need to know is that he "increased in wisdom and stature, and in favor with God and men."

It is interesting to think about Jesus growing and increasing in wisdom and favor. This means his growth was obvious and measurable. He handled himself remarkably well with the doctors of the law in the temple at the tender age of twelve. I couldn't even put two Bible thoughts together when I entered Bible college, but as a preteen Jesus amazed the theological brain-trust of his community. Suffice it to say that Jesus was the microview of the kingdom he came to establish.

The church Jesus Christ purchased on the cross and birthed on Pentecost also should reflect the nature of his kingdom. Isaiah prophetically saw that the increase of the kingdom of Messiah would have no end. Like the radiating ripple effect in a calm lake where a stone has been tossed, the nature of the kingdom of God is ever expanding and far-reaching. This being the case, there must be leaders in his kingdom who have made a personal commitment to grow.

Throughout my life I have spent time and money I did not have to attend conferences that would challenge me and help me grow as a leader. Early in my ministry I somehow understood that the number-one requisite to pastoring a growing congregation is leadership. If the leader is growing, then the congregation will grow.

In the mid-1980s I was almost thirty and desperate to do something significant for God. I attended a church growth conference in Chicago, paid the registration, and made the ninety-minute drive to the windy city. During the first six hours of that one-day conference I suffered through the two most boring speakers I've ever heard in my life talking about things that had zero relevance to my situation. I felt like the entire day and my financial sacrifice was wasted.

For the last session, however, the emcee introduced the speaker something like this: "Now our final speaker of the day is unknown to you, but his star is rising, and soon all of Christianity will have heard about this thirty-eight-year-old pastor from Lancaster, Ohio. Would you please welcome John Maxwell!" In my view, John saved the day. That sleepy audience came alive. We cheered, we cried, and we clapped. The last thirty-five minutes of that one-day seminar altered the trajectory of the next thirty-five years of my life. Not only was John a great communicator, but I was introduced to a resource of Christian leadership that has blessed my life and consequently, everyone's life around me. I had already made a commitment to grow, but that day connected my commitment to a new resource that boosted me to a new level.

It should be a universal given that if a local congregation is healthy, it will grow. I understand that not all leaders are equally gifted, and I believe that God calls pastors to lead thousands, hundreds, fifties, and tens. This was the plan Moses's father-in-law gave him to more effectively care for the church in the wilderness. Some of Moses's leaders were more skilled and gifted than others, but they all were valuable because Moses strategically placed them where they would add the most value. How ridiculous it would have been for a man gifted to lead ten to challenge the captain over a thousand for his job. That would be like a fan sitting behind the Chicago Bulls bench asking Phil Jackson if he could take the last shot instead of Michael Jordan.

If a church leader (pastor, department director) has been called, gifted, and equipped to serve thirty people, and they are faithfully and fruitfully serving God and the community, has he/she failed the Lord? A high priority has been placed on growing a megachurch, but the truth is that not every called man or woman of God is gifted to the same degree or in the same way. Nobody wins the church-growth lottery. Nobody wakes up one Sunday morning to find thousands of people flowing through the church doors.

Church leaders typically present the parable of the talents (Matthew 25) in hopes of inspiring those they lead to invest their talents, multiply them, and give a return to God for his goodness to them. However, there is an alternate interpretation that is well within the scope of the Lord's intent for his disciples, and that is to look at this parable through the lens of leading. The three servants then become church leaders, and their "talents" are those they lead.

These three leaders are given five, two, and one talent respectively. God does not love five-talented leaders more than the one-talented. His expectation is that we would give him a return for his investment in us, whether great or small. Not every leader is equipped by God to grow a megachurch, and we need to accept that. I believe God calls and equips some men to lead thousands and others to lead just a few. The question is not "How many did you have in church on Sunday?" but "Are the people under your leadership growing?"

Many years ago, I stepped into an elevator in our headquarters building and found myself standing next to the pastor of the largest congregation in our denomination. He was old enough to be my father, and I had admired him from afar my entire ministerial life. I knew our elevator conversation would have a thirty-second duration, so I quickly introduced myself. To my surprise, he said he knew who I was. Then I said, "Could I please ask you how many you had in church last Sunday?"

He humbly and thoughtfully looked down for a moment and then said, "I believe we had about thirty-eight hundred."

I smiled and responded, "Well, bishop, between you and me we had about four thousand in church last Sunday." We laughed, the doors opened, and we walked out of the elevator as if we were ministry partners.

I will never forget that Kodak moment. He has since gone to be with the Lord, but not before he built a six-thousand-seat sanctuary. How gracious he was to allow someone far less talented to share a light moment with him that made my day. Ironically, a few years later I was elected to fill the high organizational office in which he had served for many years. I keenly understand that I am not nearly as gifted a leader as he, but this fact is irrelevant in my position with God. I can only be myself; everyone else is taken. My job—and your job—is to be faithful and fruitful.

Dake's Annotated Reference Bible estimates a talent to be worth twenty-nine thousand dollars. It is easy to see that these leaders of Matthew 25 were responsible for valuable assets on loan from their master. John Maxwell once said, "People are the greatest appreciable asset in any organization of value." Who could put a price on one person in any of our congregations? As church leaders, it is incumbent upon us to assign high value to every human being that God places under our purview. Maxwell has taught us to treat everyone we meet like they are a "ten." People will figure out quickly what value we have placed on them by how we speak to them, how we treat them, and the body language we use to communicate with them. Do we speak to them condescendingly? Do we constantly look over their shoulder for someone more important to walk by? We must not see people for what we can get out of them but rather what value we can add to them.

In my home church was a man who, as a little boy, had been chronically beaten by his angry father, who would then lock him in the basement for hours on end. He even would beat him for the disobedience of his younger brother. This ongoing physical abuse resulted in some sort of mental retardation. One might wonder what value a man like this could possibly add to any organization?

This man would show up at church every time the door was open, even if it meant walking during a rainstorm. The pastor noticed this man's faithfulness and desire to do something to serve, so he gave him keys to the church and assigned him the job of opening and closing the building before and after services. He took great pride in the responsibility of his ministry and executed it perfectly.

He worked in a vehicle-repair shop. Unable to look at a clock and tell the time, he relied on his body clock to wake him up in time for work. Often, he would arrive an hour or more before the shop opened, so he would sit in his car and pray while waiting for the foreman to arrive. The boss eventually noticed his faithful early arrival and asked him if he would like to be responsible for opening the shop. He was happy to do this as it made him feel very valued.

For the next twenty-plus years he would open the shop and then go to the office, get down on his knees, and pray for the business until the boss came in. At the time he hired on, the company had only nine employees. By the time he retired, they were a multimillion-dollar company with over 160 employees. Somebody had given him a key and made him feel valuable. In turn, his life and prayers made a significant contribution to that company as well as to many families in that community. Everyone has a gift that can add value to the ministry when given a chance.

Some leaders see their church members as property or pawns; in contrast, the scripture places high value on the "saints." They are "called," and they shall "judge the world." Apostle Peter wrote that believers are "a royal priesthood, and a holy nation" (2 Pet. 2:9). What great value the apostle's inspired words place upon those whom Christ has redeemed! Peter's announcement did not originate with him, however. God envisioned that his people would be a priesthood as early as Exodus 19:5–6.

The body of Christ is done a disservice when the unbiblical polity of "clergy and laity" is in operation. The notion that the clergy are the "educated and holy" members of the congregation who sit on the platform and conduct liturgical exercises, while the laity are the "uneducated and unqualified" members who sit in the pews and nod their heads (whether in approval or slumber) is an insult to Christ's finished work on the cross. This concept is rife with problems and is a setup for dysfunction. Arguably, this paradigm of leadership is what sent the church into the Dark Ages. The adage that absolute power corrupts absolutely applies.

In the beginning it was not so. The governing ministry in the New Testament church was apostles who go, prophets who guide, evangelists who gather, pastors who grow, and teachers who ground (Ephesians 4:11). The fivefold ministry embraced mutual accountability, fulfilling their role of governing the church and equipping the saints for the work of the ministry. These early church leaders had a high view of the members of their congregations.

Apostles Paul and Peter used terminology to demonstrate great honor to faithful and fruitful saints of God: "Beloved of God, called to be saints, fellow laborer, fellow soldier, partners, a chosen generation, a royal priesthood, a holy nation," and such like. In my years of pastoring, I have never felt that church members were my personal property to be moved around like pawns on a chessboard. Christlike leaders see people as assets, not liabilities.

I have heard church leaders talk about their members as if they were slaves, imbeciles, and worse. I have heard church leaders talk down to people as if they were devoid of any intellect. A broken-hearted mother and former member of our church who moved to another town recently called me to say that her troubled twenty-something son had finally come to church with her. She was excited to have him sitting beside her in the house of God; that is, until the pastor called him out for grinning during his sermon. The pastor said, "If you think this is so funny, why don't you just get up, leave this sanctuary right now, and don't ever come back!" Without saying a word, the young man stood up and walked out.

I'm sure the pastor prided himself for putting that young man in his place. Undoubtedly this demonstration of authority struck sufficient fear into everyone else that this grievous insubordination, now effectively punished, should never be repeated; from henceforth, there shall be zero tolerance for disrespecting this man of God in this sanctuary. What the pastor didn't know is that just a few hours earlier this frantic mother had wrestled a loaded handgun out of her son's hands to prevented him from taking his life.

What would be the fallout of such an episode? Would this explosion endear the mother's heart to her pastor? Would the father write out his tithe check with great joy the next Sunday and add a little extra because the pastor had showed such love to their troubled son? Would the other church members be confident that their invited guests would be treated well and with respect should they risk a grin or an eye roll during the sermon? Would the one who called this pastor be pleased with how he handled a valuable talent that had been given to him?

This pastor obviously never heard of Dale Carnegie. His you-shut-up-and-listen philosophy inspired him to interpret the grin as disrespect when he had no idea what was behind that grin. Would this perhaps have been an opportunity to file the moment away for a future conversation with the young man? Could he have taken a ministry approach, given the boy a "pass," or just turned the other cheek? By taking him aside and showing a personal interest in his well-being, could the pastor possibly have set a positive direction for his life? Every one of us can remember a single moment where our pastor or a church leader spoke a word to us, for one reason or another, and the ensuing effect it had on our lives.

It is my observation that pastors who habitually make public examples out of church attenders are telling on themselves. While they may feel as though they are cleaning up the church, they may be revealing their insecurity, anger issues, or frustrations at home. Their idea of a good church service might conjure the imagery of Jesus angrily cleansing the temple with a whip in his hands. The angrier they get, the cleaner the church becomes. One of my elders called this leadership attitude "Fewer but purer." I once heard a speaker pose the following question: "If the words you spoke about others would ascend into heaven as a prayer and then descend on them like a wardrobe, how would the people you speak to or talk about be dressed? Would they be dressed like paupers or like royalty?"

Upon hitting a bad shot while playing golf I've been known to mutter to myself, "You dummy" or "You idiot" or "You're so stupid." Think about it: would I pay someone fifty dollars and tell him to "follow me around this golf course today, and every time I hit a bad shot, I want you to call me dummy or idiot or stupid." No, I wouldn't pay anyone else to call me those names, so why would I do that to myself?

The words we speak to others and to ourselves are powerful. The old playground rhyme "Sticks and stones may break my bones, but names will never harm me" is a lie. We all remember mean things that adults or peers said about us or to us. I recall a girl that I thought was cute making fun of how I chewed my food in a sixth-grade lunchroom. Her criticism made me extremely self-conscious. In the 1970s, all my friends in high school wore their hair past their collars, but my dad made me get a 1950s haircut every month, whether I needed it or not. One day in the hallway I was in a group of guys (mostly jocks in their letter jackets) and said something humorous that made everyone laugh. The star running back looked at me and said, "You know, Stan, you would be so cool if you didn't have such a stupid haircut." Others have suffered much worse than I, but we have all felt the sting of the tongue.

For every time a tongue has stung my spirit, there have been multiplied occasions where someone's words have blessed and encouraged me. My father's words blessed me all my life: from compliments of how well I cut the grass or shoveled the snow from our eighty-foot driveway, or playing my baritone horn well in the school band or church orchestra, to singing solos in the youth choir, to affirming a message that I preached where he was in the audience—or even when he wasn't in the audience. For instance, many years after the fact a friend told me that as he was walking down the hallway of our college and noticed that my dad had his ear pressed against the door of a classroom. Dad noticed the question on his face and pointed toward the door and with a smile explained, "Stan's speaking."

A short affirmative phrase or written note from a parent, pastor, or church leader can easily make someone's day and give them a gift that could last a lifetime. Scripture says that death and life are in the power of the tongue (Prov. 18:21, KJV). Jesus said, "The words that I speak to you are spirit, and they are life" (John 6:63).

Gary Smalley and John Trent wrote a book titled *The Blessing*. I read this life-changing revelation when my oldest son, Justin, was a newborn. Smalley and Trent unpack the biblical principle found in Genesis 27 of giving the blessing to our children. They present research that if a child does not receive the family blessing, he/she will spend a lifetime searching for it. There are five main elements to giving the blessing, one of which is "a spoken message." This is a carefully worded message of approval that is spoken directly to the child. Words like, "I'm so proud of you." "I saw what you did and you were incredible." Or simply, "I want you to know that I love you." If parents don't speak words of affirmation and instead assume their children know how they feel about them by their actions, they may spend their lives pursuing love and affirmation in the wrong places.

The Jewish culture has done a good job of speaking words of value over their children. The joke and yet a powerful message among them is introducing their young children to their colleagues as doctors or attorneys. A friend of mine who had a prolific prison ministry shared with me that one day while speaking to hundreds of convicts he asked the question "How many of you ever heard your mother or father tell you, 'You're going to end up in prison someday'?" He said nearly every one of them raised their hand. Comments made in frustration tend to prophesy futures.

The five- and two-talented church leaders understand the value of what their master has placed in their hands. They invest in people, add value to them, nurture them to health and spiritual maturity, and provide opportunities for them to grow and serve. Ultimately, they give their master a multiplied and fruitful return for his investment. One-talented church leaders can view their master through a negative lens: hard, austere, unforgiving, taking from places where he never invested, spending no time or resources on anyone's development, and leaving them sitting there doing nothing. Jesus called this kind of leader "wicked and lazy" (Matt. 25:26).

I have never understood pastors who penalize misbehaving church members (who are in leadership) with set probationary periods. It seems more Christlike to watch for a change of mind, heart, and attitude, rather than just assign someone to spiritual Alcatraz for months on end. The prodigal son of Luke 15 was immediately restored to the status of "son." The woman taken in the act of adultery was given permission to "go and sin no more." The much-married woman at the well of Samaria left her waterpot and returned with a multitude of friends who later were part of Philip's revival in Acts 8.

Jesus did not ban Peter to a dungeon for his triple denial in a crucial moment, but he informed Peter that he had anticipated his failure, had prayed for him that his faith would not fail, that he would be "converted" (have a change of heart and attitude), and then he would be profitable for the ministry by strengthening his brethren. Jesus pictured a future of restoration, value, and ownership of ministry for Peter, which undoubtedly brought him through a very dark time of self-disappointment.

How different Judas's story could have been! Judas also had betrayed the Lord, but Jesus gave him opportunity to be restored when he greeted him kindly at his arrest, even with the cold kiss of betrayal still wet on his cheek. The difference between Peter and Judas (who could argue which sin was more egregious given the implications for both), was that Peter believed in the wellness of his leader, Jesus. He understood that Jesus was reasonable, approachable, and redemptive. Conversely, Judas's internal lens apparently viewed Jesus as judgmental, intolerant, and unforgiving, and gave him no hope of redemption.

A pastor's words and actions are powerful and can either bind flawed church members to the body of Christ or lose them from the body. Church leaders must become proficient at dispensing hope. We are not responsible for those we lead, but we are responsible to help them find a pathway to recovery and peace. If we are redemptive in confrontation but they refuse to receive it and respond by doing something extreme, at least we will not bear the remorse of piling on their pain to the point of no return. If we are going to make a mistake, let's make it on the side of mercy and not judgment.

CHAPTER 14

CHRISTLIKE LEADERS FINISH WELL

I have glorified You on the earth. I have finished the work which You have given Me to do (John 17:4).

"Don't write off the next generation; no one else is coming."—Earl Creps

G od is a planner. John 1:1 says, "In the beginning was the Word, and the Word was with God, and the Word was God." *Logos* (word) includes the idea of God's thoughts, plans, and envisagement. Verse 14 says, "The Word became flesh and dwelt among us, and we beheld His glory, the glory as of the only begotten of the Father, full of grace and truth."

God was not caught off guard with man's sin. Indeed, one rabbinical scholar has suggested that the fall occurred only three hours after Eve joined Adam in Eden. The point is no matter how long it took the couple to sidle over to the forbidden tree, God had seen it coming and had a plan in place. Revelation 13:8 says the Lamb was slain from the foundation of the world. In his mind, God envisioned how he would manifest himself in flesh, dwell among his fallen

157

human creation, and redeem them. He didn't plan to send someone else to save the world; he planned to come himself.

In his message on Mars' Hill, Paul preached that God is the giver of all life and breath and all things. Life is the greatest gift. I would add that God-inspired biography is the greatest literature and therefore our greatest teacher. Paul wrote that the "Jewish laws were our teacher and guide until Christ came to give us right standing with God through our faith" (Gal. 3:24 TLB). In a letter to the Corinthians, he referenced the biographies of old: "All these things happened to them as example…they were written down so that we could read about them and learn from them" (1 Cor. 10:11, TLB).

If we consider the Bible to be a metabiography, we readily recognize it is God's story, which makes the Bible an autobiography. The heroes of our faith walked across the pages of the Bible because they played a small part in an epic story: God's story of redemption. If it were possible to cut any page of the Bible, it would bleed the red blood of Jesus Christ. Reading the Bible as one continuing narrative makes it plain that the "author and finisher of our faith" is also the "first and the last."

God declares the end from the beginning (Isaiah 46:10), which means he didn't start at creation with high hopes that everything would turn out all right at the end. God worked backward from Revelation to Genesis, keeping the end in view. Isaiah declared that God proceeded to reveal his plan line upon line, precept upon precept, here a little and there a little. God will never have to say, "Well, I didn't see that coming." He will never lose control of his agenda. The eschaton is unfolding exactly the way he planned. Only one question remains: will we follow our creator and Savior's pattern of planning with our own lives and ministries?

The scripture has a way of encapsulating years of the life of its subplots in poignant epitaphs: he died as a fool (Abner), he went to his own place (Judas), oh how the mighty have fallen (Saul), and he forsook me having loved this present world (Demas). These stinging last words that God spoke over these actors as they existed the stage of the scriptures prick my spirit every time I read them, and at times I have cringed. How will God summarize my feeble years on this earth? I can only hope my epitaph is placed somewhere in the genre that says he was a friend of God, the disciple whom Jesus loved, or he fought a good fight.

Death does not wave a mystical wand over us and suddenly transform an abject life into an honorable life. You may have heard the story of the widow at her husband's funeral, who suddenly got up during the eulogy to look in the casket just to make sure he was the one they were talking about. We all want to hear the words "Well done, good and faithful servant." Theologically, we cannot expect to hear those words unless we obey the gospel of Jesus Christ and give him a return for his investment.

Paul's personal but inspired epitaph of "I fought a good fight, I have finished my course, I have kept the faith" not only describes the best years of his ministry, but it carries us right up to his dying breath. He is dying the same way he lived, in real time. Did Timothy receive the news of Paul's death from Rome weeks later and attempt to grieve amid his mad scramble to try and figure out what Paul wanted done after his exit? No, Paul intentionally communicated with his successor right up to the end, and celebrated his timely handoff.

How do we know Paul planned his exit? The scripture names seventeen of his personal disciples, who in turn made thirty other named disciples. Paul had forty-seven trained, equipped, empowered, and released successors on his discipleship tree. He established elders in the churches he planted and successfully made the handoff to the next generation.

Before there can be a successful leadership transition, according to the model of David, every new leader must receive three anointings: David was anointed by God, then by Samuel, and finally by the people. Even though God has called you, and the church board or elders have approved you, and now you have been elected or wear the title of "Pastor" (or insert any church-related title), it does not automatically follow that you are now the leader. The people may have voted for you because the elders approved you, but they will not anoint you until you have proven yourself to them.

I understand that local churches are either congregational in their polity or hierarchal, but the biblical passage of transition seems to be that a sitting well-tenured pastor should have a profound influence on who should be the next pastor. A pastor invests his life in the congregation and community. His DNA and fingerprints are on every surface. The church knows its identity and its mission, and it knows how to get the job done. Why invite some unknown leader from a completely foreign church culture to come in and turn everything upside down, particularly if the church is functioning well and on mission? It would seem wiser, more prudent, smoother, and more sensible to have someone groomed and ready, who knows the congregation and its inner workings, and is poised to take everything to a new level.

Paul shared his pattern with his son in the gospel, Timothy, when he wrote, "And the things that you have heard from me among many witnesses, commit these to faithful men who will be able to teach others also." Embedded in this single verse are four generations with three handoffs. Paul did not hang on until everything around him began to deteriorate, wither, and die. He left his legacy by believing in and making room for the next generation of apostolic leaders.

He derived this concept from Jesus—you know, the one we are following. Jesus is not just our Savior and our example in kindness, love, and character; he is our example in everything, including our finish. He planned for his exit from day one. He chose twelve disciples "to be with him" to train, mentor, share, invest, empower, and release to succeed him. He continually told them he was going away, but they didn't understand that statement until it actually happened. In John 14:12 he said, "You not only are going to do the works I am doing, but you are going to do greater works! And then I am going to leave it with you."

What shape would the church be in today if Jesus hadn't trained anyone to succeed him? What if his only exit strategy was to die on the cross without building a team that would outlive him? What if his thinking was "I'm just going to do my thing and let them figure it out when I'm gone"? What if Jesus had spent time with the multitude only on Sundays (like fish-and-chips Sunday in John 6) and built no relationships? John Maxwell says "There is no success without a successor." That's not in the Bible, but perhaps it ought to be. The concept, however, is interwoven throughout the scripture.

I must ask a hard question: what shape would every congregation in America be in right now if every church leader and/or pastor clung tightly to their position until they turned eighty-five? How about seventy-five? Or seventy? Jesus didn't walk the road of sorrow to Calvary when he was old and stooped and unsteady on his feet. He didn't do his greatest work on the cross when his mind was dulled, his voice was weak, and the light in his eyes was growing dim. He poured out his life for us and successfully made his transition when he was on top of his game, and not just a shell of his former self.

Now that I'm into my sixties, I've been thinking more often about my legacy, asking myself questions like, "What have I done with my life that will outlive me?" "Who have I touched that is better for it?" "Did I leave a trail of bodies behind or a wake of hale and hearty followers?" "What will be said about me after I am gone?" "At my funeral will my colleagues speak glowingly of me publicly but privately stroke their chins and whisper to each other, 'Too bad he hung on too long'?" Will I listen to my family or close friends about the timing of my resignation more than I listen to God? Will I follow through on my transition plans and the promises I made to God, to myself, and to my church leaders, or will I succumb as countless others before me, to the ode of "Just One More Sunday in the Saddle"?

It is satisfying to be able to say, "All's well that ends well," but this phrase typically means (1) we didn't plan, (2) we gave it little forethought, (3) we flew by the seat of our pants, (4) we winged it and faked, hoping to make it, or (5) our finish was greatly in doubt until, by an unforeseen event of divine intervention, we finally pulled it off at the last moment. To use a baseball analogy, your team is down by three runs, you need four to win, it's the bottom of the ninth, two outs, bases are loaded, it's a full count, and "Casey's at bat." Does this sound like an appropriate exit strategy for a seasoned man or woman of God? As an avid observer of countless church leaders in the throes of transition, particularly lead/senior pastors, too many long-tenured pastors have snatched defeat from the jaws of victory. You never have to recover from a good start.

A true man of God always places the welfare of the congregation before personal considerations in every decision, even regarding his personal finances. Most pastors have disciplined themselves to make sure the church bills are paid before they receive any remuneration. As proper and admirable as this attitude is, it often leaves the pastor unprepared for retirement. Too many pastors have remained at the helm long after their health, energy, vision, and ability to effectively communicate has significantly diminished. Because they have not prepared financially for retirement, they continue to collect paychecks while everything deteriorates around them. In organizations with self-governing congregations, no one wants to step in, be the bad guy, and suggest a resignation. It is heartbreaking to stand on the sidelines and watch solid and thriving congregations diminish with the aging of their pastor.

Sometimes our theology hurts us. I am a strong advocate of premillennialism, including the imminent return of Christ. With that in mind, I have watched other strong advocates of this eschatological view lose balance and completely ignore financial planning because Jesus is coming soon. We well know the wide range of predictions about the time of Christ's return. Books and videos have been sold, movies produced, and many Christians have been stirred, made plans, sold possessions, and changed their behavior, only to become bitterly disappointed. Some got tired of waiting and have even departed from the faith.

This is not a book about the eschaton so I will not argue for my viewpoint. But there remains the isolated notion that financial planning is unspiritual and eliminates trust in God. After all, Jesus told us not to worry about what tomorrow will bring, and if he takes care of birds and lilies then he will take care of us. That sounds sacred enough to have a moment of silence right now, but that's not all the scripture says about the future.

Moses and David prepared financially to build their houses of God. They did not forge ahead haphazardly, hoping somebody would show up with an offering. Moses cast vision to build the tabernacle in the wilderness, and the vision was so compelling that he had to restrain the congregation from giving more because they had more than enough. I've never seen this, have you? First Chronicles 22:5 says that before his death, David prepared abundantly for building the temple. All was not well because it ended well, but all was well because it began well.

When the work of the second temple had been stalled for twenty years, God stirred up the prophet Zechariah to speak into Governor Zerubbabel's life to finish the work. God uttered the famous declaration, "It is not by might, nor by power, but by my Spirit says the Lord." Then he said that the mountain (i.e., the project) before them would be leveled like a plain, and when they brought the capstone, they would shout, "Grace did it!" They went about raising money, assembling skilled workers, and preparing to get the work done.

The Year of Jubilee was God's way of recalibrating the nation of Israel's economy every fifty years. Everything reset to zero: debt was forgiven, slaves were released, and land went back to the original family. Unfortunately, there is no record that Israel ever celebrated this institution, perhaps because of greed and lack of planning. Neither did Israel ever celebrate the sabbatical year. Every seventh year the land was to rest, replenish, and rejuvenate. God promised them a bumper crop in the sixth harvest year, lasting through the sabbatical year and into the planting and harvest season of the new cycle of year one. Through 490 years of history there is no record that Israel celebrated the sabbatical year, so God took it from them during their seventy-year exile in Babylon. They were greedy, living hand-to-mouth, not trusting God and his financial strategy for their future, so God stepped in and rearranged things according to his plan.

Proverbs 13:22 says that "a good man leaves an inheritance to his children's children." We should lay up enough of an inheritance that it extends beyond a nice vacation for our kids after we are gone. There should be enough to bless our grandchildren. Anyone can do this. This is not an income issue, but it is an issue of intentionally planning to save. A twenty-five-year-old who starts saving twenty-five dollars per week (forgoing five lattes) can turn it into a cool one million dollars by the time they retire. I am no Dave Ramsey; I'm just a simple but intentional church leader who passionately desires to finish well and leave the next generation in better shape than what was handed to me.

I'm a baby boomer, a member of the generation that seems to be in denial of its mortality. Author Earl Creps agrees. In his excellent book *Off-Road Disciplines* he wrote, "Hair implants, vitamin elixirs, Botox injections, exercise machines…if the Rolling Stones can still tour, maybe there is hope for us."[16] He went on to say that Boomers lead 60 percent of America's churches. In a sobering reference, he quoted Bill Easum who said, "In another fifty years, Christianity will have about the same influence in the US as it does in Canada or Europe." Creps followed with "Walking the streets of northern Europe, passing one darkened house of worship after another, touring cities in which the odds of meeting a Christ follower hover around one in a hundred, I find Easum's prediction taking on a frightening reality."[17]

Let's be honest. Some church leaders cannot let go because they love the feel of power. This is not at all like Jesus. Our great example was always giving his power away. If anyone had earned the right to hang on, it was he. Creps said, "Passing the baton begins in the heart with loving the handing off more than the holding on."[18] He concluded his argument for believing in, loving, and trusting the next generation with the sobering wakeup call: "Because no one else is coming!"[19]

Here's what it comes down to: how did any of us have a chance when we started out? Either someone believed in us enough to give us a chance, or our predecessor did such a bad job he/she was either fired or resigned, or he/she became so aged there was no other choice but to resign because of declining health. The glory of dying with one's boots on may be a romanticized view of the Wild West, but who wants to be like Tombstone now?

Too many young ministers have fallen prey to broken promises by elders who just couldn't let go. George Barna said of the baby

---

[16] Earl Creps, *Off-Road Disciplines* (San Francisco: Jossey-Bass, 2006), 181.
[17] Ibid., 175.
[18] Ibid., 176.
[19] Ibid., 184.

boomer generation, "The sticking point is our core value: power. We love power. We live for power. Power lunches, power ties, power suits, power offices, power titles, power cars, power networks… Boomers revel in power. The sad result is that most Boomers, even those in the pastorate or in voluntary, lay-leadership positions in churches, have no intention of lovingly handing the baton to Baby Busters."[20]

Jesus placed as much faith in his successors as he did in himself. Perhaps the most tender picture we see of his expressed faith in and love for them is the narrative of the Last Supper recorded in John 13. We can learn from this pivotal moment when Jesus was ready to take the next transitional step. He had taught them in the hillside class-rooms of Judea, Samaria, and Galilee, and trained them by sending them out by twos to test their wings. He had then called them back for a time of assessment and accountability. Jesus was not a one-man show with a Cub Scout troop following him around like baby bears, becoming so enamored with their praise that he just couldn't make himself pass the baton. He celebrated them more than they cele-brated him.

John 13:1 says that Jesus knew his hour had come. It was time for him to leave. Verse 3 says, "Jesus, knowing that the Father had given all things into His hands, and that He had come from God, and was going to God, rose from supper, and laid aside His garments, took a towel and girded Himself." This powerfully reveals Jesus's lack of insecurity; Jesus could hand off the baton because he knew who he was, where he had come from, and where he was going. This is key to making a successful transition and exposes why some are seemingly unwilling to do so.

What emotional toll did it take for Jesus to say, "It is finished"? For some reason, those words get stuck in our throats. Hangers-on would argue with Jesus even as he is on the cross, "Surely there are more miracles to work, more sermons to preach, and more disci-ples to make. So what do you mean by saying, 'It's finished'? You're only thirty-three years old. Why, if we were your age, we would have another forty years or more of expert leading!"

---

[20] "Gracefully Passing the Baton" (*Barna Update,* Apr. 26, 2004).

These "Johnny-leave-latelys" would most likely would fuss with Paul about his declaration of finishing his course. "What are you talking about, Paul? You are *the* apostle to the Gentiles! The Gentile revival needs you. No one else can do it but you. Surely there are more continents to open, more churches to plant, more disciples to make, more letters to write, and more miracles to perform. How dare you say, 'My course is finished'?"

Paul took his cue from his Savior, Jesus Christ. Jesus didn't say, "I am finished," and neither did Paul. Jesus said, "It is finished," and Paul said, "I have finished." They well understood the difference between the end of their lives and the handoff of their ministry. If they didn't capture the moment to complete the handoff, then the choice would have been taken out of their hands. They intuitively recognized they had arrived in the critical handoff zone. There is a window of time when all leaders come to the handoff zone, and we better know when we reach it and what we are supposed to do once we get there. We would all do well to understand that there's never enough time to do *our* will, but there always will be enough time to do the will of God.

Who are you training right now to succeed you? If you are fifty years old or more, don't wait another day to get started. God is interested, if not motivated, to reveal to you who your successor should be. For example, he spoke clearly to Elijah one day about his successor and even included his name and where he could find him. I won't attempt to unpack the whole Elijah/Elisha handoff, but I must mention one unique feature. When Elijah informed his protégé that he was leaving, he asked him what he wanted from him. Elisha boldly requested a double portion of his spirit. Elijah's response was, "You have asked a hard thing. Nevertheless, if you see me when I am taken from you, it shall be so for you; but if not, it shall not be so" (2 Kings 2:10).

Perhaps Elijah was saying, "Elisha, when you see eye to eye with me, you shall have what you asked for." Assuredly, transitions can be tricky, but I would say the key of a successful handoff is for Elisha to see what Elijah sees. Israel did not need Elisha to think like a farmer, act like a plowman, speak like an ox driver, or see well enough to plow a straight row; God's people needed Elisha to think, act, speak, and see like their prophet. As soon as Elijah was sure that Elisha "had it," he was gone.

Jesus was prepared to die on the cross. Twice he said he had finished. The second time is much more famous, since it was uttered on the cross. The first time was during his priestly prayer in John 17:4, but it was no less dramatic. He prayed, "I have finished the work which you have given me to do." What work was this? His magnificent work on the cross? Not yet. This was the work of making disciples and establishing his successors. We know this because his prayer is centered on his work with them and interceding for their work in the world. Thirty-two times Jesus mentioned those he trained to carry on the mission of making disciples of all nations, and some forty times Jesus leveraged the tension that the world would impose upon them as they executed their mission.

When Jesus was ready to exit, he had finished his work, both pragmatically and theologically. He did not have any loose ends to tie up, unless you think assigning the care of his mother to John qualified as a loose end. Josh McDowell calculated that within the last twenty-four hours of his life Jesus fulfilled twenty-nine messianic prophesies.[21] He was taking care of business, and there were no unresolved emotional issues to confront. He did not have any proverbial axes to grind. He had already prayed, "Nevertheless, not my will, but yours be done."

I am convinced that some church leaders can't let go because of unresolved emotional issues. They may feel as though they owe someone something or that someone has something to lose if they let go of the reins. Emotions are wonderful to display at weddings, funerals, anniversaries, and birthdays, but they hold too many people hostage who need to move on to the next season of their life.

When I was thirty-nine, I captured an image in my mind and spirit I will never forget. My dear father had come to the end of his journey. Mom and my siblings Gary, Pat, and Pam, were gath-

---

[21] Josh McDowell, *Evidence That Demands a Verdict* (Nashville, TN: Thomas Nelson, 2017).

ered around his bedside. He had fought long and hard for five years against cancer. His formerly bright eyes were now sunken, and his always-smiling cheeks were now hollow. His hands were shaking, and his voice was soft and raspy. He looked around at the five of us and spoke the priestly blessing over us: "The Lord bless you and keep you, the Lord make his face to shine upon you, and be gracious unto you. The Lord set his countenance upon you and give you peace."

It was a holy moment, a sanctuary. The presence of God was there. The greatest Christlike man I had ever known had finished well. There were no apologizes necessary to offer or receive. There were no hatchets to bury or axes to grind. All accounts were settled. There were no elephants skulking in the room. Nobody sobbed uncontrollably due to unresolved emotional issues. It was gentle, peaceful, merciful, and glorious. I will cherish that memory forever.

I decided in that moment that I want to finish in the same way. I want to be married to the same woman for over fifty years. I want my wife and children to love and respect me more than any of my colleagues (none of them will be there to hold my hand). I want to finish, knowing that my offspring have lived out my values and successfully handed them over to their children. I want to know that everything I spent my life building is going to a new level and not going down with my departure.

Who is your son or daughter in the faith? Have you transmitted your spiritual DNA to anyone? Who sings like you, prays like you, worships God like you, leads like you, preaches or teaches like you, or makes disciples like you? Are you going to be a one-and-done church leader or are you going to finish well? If you *are* going to finish well, you must have that son or daughter now in relationship. They are worthy of your investment to pray over, love, and involve them right now. Why? "Because no one else is coming!"

ABOUT THE AUTHOR

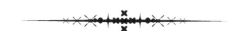

S tan O. Gleason has served as lead pastor of the Life Church of Kansas City, Missouri, for over thirty years. Together with his wife of forty-three years, Marlene, they have raised four children who are all engaged in ministry. He is the author of *Follow to Lead: The Journey of a Disciple-Maker*. He earned an MA from Urshan Graduate School of Theology and a BA from Apostolic Bible Institute. He also currently serves as assistant general superintendent of United Pentecostal Church International.

CPSIA information can be obtained
at www.ICGtesting.com
Printed in the USA
BVHW080309110123
655987BV00002B/158

9 781685 176631